Compliments of
A.D. Amar, Editor
Mid-Atlantic Journal of Busines

D1225265

DATE DUE

The Art of Bargaining

Richard Ned Lebow

The Art of
Bargaining

THE JOHNS HOPKINS UNIVERSITY PRESS • BALTIMORE & LONDON

© 1996 The Johns Hopkins University Press
All rights reserved. Published 1996
Printed in the United States of America on acid-free paper

05   04   03   02   01   00   99   98   97   96   5   4   3   2   1

The Johns Hopkins University Press
2715 North Charles Street
Baltimore, Maryland 21218-4319
The Johns Hopkins Press Ltd., London

ISBN 0-8018-5198-X

Library of Congress Cataloging-in-Publication Data will be found at the end of this book.

A catalog record for this book is available from the British Library.

To my son David,

who taught me everything I know

about the art of bargaining

Contents

PART 3 · A BARGAIN IS JUST THE BEGINNING

PART 4 · PROBLEM SHOOTING

Preface

In 1992, I assumed responsibility for teaching a five-week module on bargaining at the University of Pittsburgh's Graduate School of Public and International Affairs. I searched in vain for a basic text that would acquaint task-oriented students with the fundamentals of bargaining. I had to rely on my lectures to do the job. Those lectures, revised in response to reactions from students and other readers, form the basis of this book. They draw on my personal and professional experience of bargaining and use examples from widely varying circumstances to illustrate the principles of bargaining.

Bookstores and library shelves bulge with primers on bargaining. The popular literature can be divided roughly into two camps. The first of these reflects the values and aspirations of the 1960s. Its authors rebel against conceptions of bargaining as confrontation in which the more powerful party is able to impose its terms. They are uncomfortable with conflict and inequality and espouse approaches based on openness and empathy that emphasize the mutual benefits of agreement. They encourage readers to design so-called "win-win" strategies that reward both sides in any bargaining encounter. Such an accommodative approach to bargaining has real value, but its advocates generally exaggerate the extent to which goodwill, reason, and imagination can bridge real differences of interest and imbalances of power or triumph over greed, stubbornness, anger, and misunderstanding.

Other bargaining books reflect the zeitgeist of the 1980s. They emphasize "winning" and strategies intended to produce the most favorable outcomes. Advocates of the "kick them while they're down" approach to bargaining scorn softness and unnecessary compromise and urge readers to think in a hard-nosed way about their interests and how they can be

protected or advanced in a conflictual and competitive world. This literature might provide a useful corrective to the overly optimistic mind-set of
win-win bargaining if it did not go overboard in the opposite direction. It
is ludicrous to assume that everybody you encounter is always motivated
by the most narrow conceptions of self-interest and intent on exploiting
any sign of weakness or seeming naivete. Competitive strategies clearly
have their uses, but they can be counterproductive when they provoke
hostility, poison important relationships, or make worst-case assessments
of other's motives self-fulfilling.

The best-known book on bargaining, *Getting to Yes,* holds out the
promise of finessing the choice between competitive and accommodative
strategies. Its authors, Roger Fisher and Harold Ury, offer "principled
bargaining" as a workable alternative. Fisher and Ury urge readers to
identify the interests of the two sides and to design an outcome that, as far
as possible, satisfies those interests. Differences that remain are to be
bridged by compromise. This compromise should be based on "objective
criteria," that is, on some standard that both sides and others will recognize as fair. The bargainer who proposes such an outcome or compromise
should refuse to alter its terms in response to threats, rewards, or other
blandishments. Fisher and Ury maintain that treating people well and
presenting offers based on principle and backed by logic are likely to
succeed. If this approach fails, readers should terminate negotiations and
execute their previously planned best alternative.

Getting to Yes really represents an awkward composite of the accommodative and competitive strategies. Its plea to come up with an offer
that meets the needs of both sides is straight off-the-shelf accommodative
bargaining. In declaring that "principled" bargainers walk away from the
table rather than haggle over terms, the authors are espousing a quintes-
sentially competitive strategy. Fisher and Ury do not conceive of nonsettlement as a coercive threat—although that is what it is—but as a prelude to
pursuing one's interests by other means. But even this use of nonsettlement
depends on a favorable power balance. Only someone who has a viable
alternative and is therefore not dependent on an agreement can walk away
from the table. "Principled bargaining" would be ludicrous in a famine,
where the cost of rejecting an offer of food at an exorbitant price would
be starvation. Fisher and Ury rely very much on the role of power in
bargaining, although it is unacknowledged and introduced through the
back door.

Getting to Yes urges readers to think about their interests but not about their power. This is helpful to the extent that it encourages people to view a bargain as a means to an end and not an end in itself. However, interest-based bargaining will fail when the parties involved have clashing interests. Suppose a sneaker manufacturer and the retail chain that markets its products each relies on a 30 percent markup to make a reasonable profit, but the market is so depressed that stores must lower their prices to move any sneakers. In this circumstance, neither manufacturer nor retailer can realize its expected 30 percent. One or both must agree to settle for less. At first glance, the fair solution might appear to be an equal reduction in their respective markups. But what if the retailer rejects this proposal as inequitable, on the grounds that its cost of doing business is proportionately higher? With a smaller profit margin, it will only break even if it has to sell sneakers at a reduced 15 percent markup. The manufacturer counters with the argument that sneakers are merely one of the products sold by the retailer and that, as other merchandise is moving well, the retailer could more easily get by with less profit from the sale of sneakers than could the manufacturer, who makes only sneakers and thus has a correspondingly greater need to make a profit on their sale.

"Principled bargaining" is also no help in the opposite circumstance: when fortune smiles on the manufacturer and retailer alike because every other teenage boy thinks that he will be scorned by his peers unless he comes to school in the new model of basketball sneaker. Stores that sell these hot shoes at a 50 percent markup cannot get enough of them to keep up with demand. "Principled bargaining" ignores this problem and offers no guidance to manufacturer and retailer for allocating what in this case is excess profit. As these simple examples indicate, there are rarely "objectively fair standards" by which to assign surplus or sacrifice. This is why people bargain.

The popular literature on bargaining is largely devoted to strategy and tactics. Strategy and tactics are important, but they are only the tip of the bargaining iceberg. What lies underneath—assessments of interests, how interests are best advanced, and the expected utility of accommodations with other parties—is more important but rarely discussed. Assessments of interests—yours and the other side's—should determine the attractiveness of bargaining, the nature of the accommodation sought, and the choice of strategy. Bargains are intended to attain broader ends, and strategies are meant to facilitate bargains. The ends should determine the choice of means.

Viewed in this light, there is nothing intrinsically good or bad about competitive, accommodative, or even "principled" bargaining. Strategies can be evaluated only in terms of the tasks they are expected to perform. Competitive bargaining is most appropriate when it is important to get the best possible deal. Accommodative bargaining is more relevant when striking a bargain is at least as important as the terms of that bargain. Many situations require a mix of strategies. This book examines the logical connections among interests, bargains, and strategies. With a clear conception of your interests, you can determine the kinds of bargains that advance those interests and the strategies most likely to bring about those bargains.

All the really important decisions about bargaining are made—or should be made—away from the negotiating table. The first two parts of this book are, accordingly, devoted to the broader context of bargaining. They compare bargaining to other methods of protecting and advancing interests and look at the different kinds of bargains and the feasibility of attaining them. This analysis should help you identify your interests more effectively and determine the extent to which bargaining is appropriate to your circumstances.

Most bargaining books assume that bargaining ends when agreement is reached. Some agreements are indeed simple to execute. When you buy a used car, you receive the vehicle, keys, and registration in return for a certified check. With luck, you never see the former owner again. Other agreements require elaborate implementation. A typical divorce settlement is likely to have clauses concerning financial assets, property, child support, and visitation rights. It needs a sustained commitment by both sides to make it work. Students of family law report that more than half of all divorce agreements involving spousal or child support are not honored for more than three years. The civil court dockets are filled with cases of businesses being sued for noncompliance with contracts. Cease-fire agreements and peace treaties are also notoriously precarious.

The fact of the matter is that agreements sometimes represent only the first stage of bargaining. Bargainers may need the support of third parties to gain ratification or implementation of their agreements. Obtaining such support may require bargaining as extensive and difficult as was necessary to secure the original agreement. Implementation may require further bargaining with the other side or with third parties if ambiguities appear or new issues arise, or if either side loses its interest in the agreement. The 1994 peace accord between Israel and the Palestine Liberation Organization illustrates all of these problems. Israeli and Palestinian negotiators expected to wrap up the remaining issues in a matter of weeks after signature of the agreement. In practice, it took them months of tough bargaining with one another and their respective constituencies to secure an agreement. As this book goes to press, powerful factions in Israel, the West Bank, and Gaza are doing their best to prevent implementation of the agreement.

Ratification and implementation follow on agreement, but it is a great mistake to postpone their consideration until after agreement has been reached. Clever negotiators anticipate ratification and implementation problems and adopt bargaining strategies and goals that may minimize them. Part 3 of this book examines impediments to ratification and implementation and what can be done during the course of bargaining to overcome them.

Attempts to strike bargains sometimes fail because interests are incompatible, or at least appear to be. Bargaining can also fail because one or both sides misjudge the other's preferences or misunderstand its signals or offers. Most treatments of bargaining assume perfect information or, failing that, perfect understanding of whatever information is available. As any experienced bargainer knows, these conditions are rarely met. People often lack critical information about the context of the bargaining or about the other side's preferences or they misinterpret what information they do have. Another important feature of this book is its analysis of why people misunderstand each other's interests and preferences and what can be done to reduce such misunderstanding. Many of my examples are drawn from international relations, where miscalculations and misjudgments are particularly rife. But the lessons of these cases are equally applicable to domestic bargaining, where the same kinds of problems regularly impede agreement.

Many bargaining books resemble cookbooks. They hold out the prospect of successful bargains if the reader follows their step-by-step recipe. But cookbooks, even good ones, rarely offer any guidance about the most fundamental of cooking decisions: the nature of the meal to be prepared. In practice, this will depend on the season, availability of foods, number of guests, their tastes and dietary restrictions, and how much time, money, and interest the chef has. A cookbook can do no more than alert would-be chefs to the need to select menus that reflect their interests, needs, finances, and abilities. This is equally true of bargaining books. They can sensitize readers to the relationships among interests, strategies, and bargaining goals and to the most common kinds of practical and communications problems they are likely to encounter. A grasp of the logical structure of bargaining and some knowledge of its fine details through exposure to examples make for better bargainers. But readers still need to use their intellect and imagination to work through their interests and choose and apply strategies and tactics described in this work to bargaining situations they confront. There are no simple, easy to follow recipes.

Introduction

Social relations are characterized by exchange. People routinely share their labor, possessions, and themselves with others. Sometimes they make gifts and ask for nothing in return. More commonly, they entertain some expectation of reciprocity. This can be tacit and ill defined: people who help their neighbors expect those neighbors to help them if the need arises. In other situations, the terms of exchange are explicit: A commuter puts down a set sum of coins on the kiosk counter and walks off with a morning newspaper. The price is well established and the only interaction between the newsagent and the commuter may be a nod of the head or a polite "good morning." Bargaining is necessary when the terms of exchange are not predetermined and any attempt to establish them reveals the clashing preferences of the parties concerned. Bargaining is communication designed to promote a satisfactory exchange.

Almost anything can be the object of bargaining. People offer goods for services or vice versa, or goods or services for money. Their bargains can be tacit or explicit. Tacit bargains avoid unpleasant haggling or the discomfort and embarrassment that may arise from admitting that a bargain has been struck. A senator who receives an honorary degree from a state university may become friendlier to higher education and back a bill to increase federal funding for student loans. If asked, the university president and the senator would vociferously deny that any deal had been struck.

Tacit bargains court misunderstanding. A man who invites a woman to an expensive dinner may expect her to go to bed with him afterwards.

The woman may have assumed that the invitation was made with no strings attached. The misunderstanding may have unpleasant consequences for both parties. Tacit bargains are made in reference to accepted social norms. When those norms become controversial or undergo rapid evolution, as has happened in the case of male-female relations, tacit bargaining becomes difficult and problematic.

To avoid misunderstandings, people often make their expectations of reciprocity explicit. Contracts go a step further and attempt to make these expectations binding. Contracts can be relatively short and straightforward, like most bills of sale. Others are extraordinarily long and complex. Corporate mergers and arms control treaties not only set out terms of exchange but usually incorporate clauses about the timing and manner of exchange, mechanisms for verification, penalties for noncompliance, and procedures for dealing with alleged violations. The Mining Provisions of the Law of Sea Treaty comprise 320 articles and 9 annexes. The all-time winner may be the 1994 General Agreement on Tariffs and Trade (GATT), which is some 22,000 pages long!

Explicit bargaining also has drawbacks. Corporate lawyers and arms control negotiators can become so concerned with protecting the interests of their principals that they are unable to reach an agreement that is clearly in the interests of both parties. The START II arms control agreement between Russia and the United States only became possible when political leaders on both sides intervened directly in the negotiations, which were deadlocked because of disputes over fine points of verification.

Explicit bargaining is paradoxical. It is conflictual behavior intended to bring about cooperation. The conflict can become acute and endanger the prospect of agreement, its implementation, or the relationship between the parties. Because of this danger, many societies surround bargaining with rituals designed to transform exchange from a confrontational to an integrative activity. Bargaining ritual often stipulates that successful encounters culminate in the sharing of food and drink, two of the most elemental forms of bonding. The rug seller buys the purchaser a coffee in the market café, two industrial executives might share a bottle of champagne after closing a big deal. Lawyers (who are less demonstrative and bill for their time) will at least shake hands.

Bargaining is deeply embedded in a broader social context. That context determines its significance, the strategies bargainers employ, and the kinds of agreements they find acceptable. The really critical decisions about bargaining should not be made at the negotiating table. Those decisions—whether or not to bargain, what kind of bargain to seek, and what strategy to employ—should be shaped by broader interests and made well before any bargaining begins.

Part 1 of this book therefore addresses the context of bargaining. Chapter 1 describes the nature of bargaining and the situations to which it is appropriate. Bargaining is a strategy, and a strategy is a means to an end. It is imperative to think about ends before choosing means. Chapter 2 examines the relationship between bargaining and the goals it is intended to achieve and the advantages and drawbacks of bargaining in comparison to other strategies that might be used toward the same ends. The decision to bargain also requires a judgment about its feasibility. Chapter 3 offers guidelines to help make such estimates. Chapter 4 walks the reader step by step through two cases of prenegotiation to illustrate how the concepts developed in this section may be applied.

Part 2 explores the strategies and tactics of bargaining. Chapters 6 through 8 analyze three strategies: coordination, rewards, and punishment. The chapters describe the distinctive character of each of the strategies, evaluate their advantages and drawbacks, and identify the situations in which they are likely to be most effective. They also look at how these strategies can be used in combination. To varying degrees, all three strategies exploit bargaining asymmetries, and Chapter 9 examines the nature of these asymmetries and how to achieve and use them effectively.

Agreements, too, are means to ends. They will not serve those ends if they cannot be implemented successfully. Part 3 explores the connection between bargaining and implementation. Chapters 10 and 11 examine obstacles to ratification and implementation and develop strategies for overcoming them. Most of these strategies need to be considered or even implemented before any agreement is reached. They should inform the course of bargaining and the choice of goals and bargaining strategies.

Carl von Clausewitz, the great Prussian philosopher of war, wrote that everything in war is simple but that simple things can be very difficult. This certainly holds true for bargaining; conceptual understanding does not necessarily translate into successful practice. Between theory and execution, many things can go wrong. One or both sides can fail to grasp their interests, can establish bargaining goals unrelated to their interests, adopt strategies or tactics counterproductive to their bargaining goals, or misinterpret the interests, signals, or offers of the other side. Chapters 12 and 13, in Part 4, address some of these problems; they examine generic causes of faulty assessment and misunderstanding and offer suggestions about how they can be avoided or corrected. Both chapters emphasize the determining and often distorting role played by the frames of reference people bring to bargaining encounters.

A final chapter offers some concluding observations about bargaining and good bargainers.

The Structure of Bargaining

The plan of this book parallels the structure of bargaining. It begins with a consideration of interests and proceeds through the selection of bargaining goals and strategies to the process of bargaining and the ratification and implementation of agreements. These stages and the steps associated with them are described below in checklist form. They provide an overview of the architecture of bargaining.

Prebargaining

1. *What is the problem?* What is the nature of the problem? Can I resolve it in isolation, or does it require (or allow) me to address other problems as well?
2. *What are my interests?* What do I have at stake on and off the table in this negotiation? Which interests are essential?
3. *What are my bargaining goals?* What do I want out of the negotiations? What am I prepared to settle for?
4. *Is bargaining feasible?* What are the interests and goals of the other side? Is there likely to be enough overlap with mine to warrant bargaining?

Bargaining

5. *Select a bargaining strategy.* Given the nature of the bargaining situation, which strategy is most appropriate? Should I use it alone or in tandem with another strategy?
6. *Increase your leverage.* What resources and advantages do I have? What can I do to increase my advantages, diminish the other side's advantages, or convince the other side of my advantages?
7. *Frame a proposal.* What kind of offer or counteroffer do I want to make? How is it conditioned by my bargaining strategy?

8. *Explain and justify your demands.* Why are my demands legitimate and reasonable?
9. *Pin down important details.* Do I want an agreement in principle or an agreement in detail? Have I reached a written agreement on all details that are important to me?

Postbargaining

10. *Ratify the agreement.* Does my agreement need ratification? What kind of terms will I need to gain ratification? Is there anything else I can do to increase the chances of ratification?
11. *Implement the agreement.* Is my agreement self-executing? If not, what requirements does it have? Have I secured those requirements in my agreement, in so far as it is possible to do so?

For purposes of analysis, it makes good sense to treat bargaining as a logical process that progresses in an orderly way from the general to the particular through reasonably well demarcated stages. But practice can differ in two important respects.

Many choices and operations overlap. Chapter 4 describes a mayor's efforts to keep a professional ball team from relocating to another city. To determine the feasibility of bargaining, the mayor had to consider his alternatives (prebargaining), select his bargaining strategy (bargaining), and determine the best way of handling a dominant constituency (ratification). He had to do all of this at the same time.

Bargaining sometimes resembles a series of feedback loops. Even when bargaining decisions are made sequentially, the outcome of any stage of bargaining can prompt reconsideration of decisions made at earlier stages. New information about the motives and goals of other parties can have the same effect. A court decision in another case can radically alter the balance of power between parties, causing one of them to reassess its interests, bargaining goals, and strategy. A president can meet unexpected opposition in the Senate to an agreement that he was on the verge of signing and have to reopen negotiations to satisfy the objections of Senate opponents. Choices and operations not only overlap, they are interdependent.

As you work your way through the chapters and their related checklists, you need to keep these relationships in mind. At the end of each bargaining stage, ask yourself how the outcome affects your previous decisions. Does it confirm or confound your expectations? Do you need to rethink your interests, goals, or strategies? Or, can you proceed to the next stage?

Part I The Nature of Bargaining

Chapter 1

What Is Bargaining?

Bargaining is a search for advantage through accommodation. When people, organizations, or states bargain, they try to glean information about others' preferences, influence their estimates of their own preferences, and exchange proposals in search of mutually acceptable agreements.

Three conditions are essential to productive bargaining:

1. *The parties involved must believe that their interests would be served by an agreement.* If one party believes that it would be better off without an agreement, it has no incentive to bargain. A separating husband who owns or controls the couple's financial assets may have no interest in negotiating a settlement with his spouse which would compel him to give up some of those assets. If he wants to remarry and needs a divorce, he will have a strong incentive to settle.

   It is often unclear beforehand if agreement will serve one's interests. The attractiveness of an agreement may depend on its terms. For this reason, bargaining in a way that gains information about the other side's preferences and the likely shape of any agreement is frequently advisable. Based on this information, you can make a more definitive decision whether to continue bargaining or to pursue your interests by other means. In 1986–87, neither the United States nor Canada was convinced that a free trade agreement would be in their respective interests. Both governments were nevertheless willing to explore the possibility of an agreement, and in the course of the negotiations they discovered that a mutually advantageous one was possible. Just the opposite happened in the Israeli-Egyptian negotiations on Palestinian autonomy initiated in 1978 by Jimmy Carter. After exploratory discussions with Egypt and the United States, Israeli leaders decided that any agreement would be contrary to their interests, and they refused to discuss the issue any further.

2. *The parties must have conflicting preferences about the terms of that agreement.* If both sides want the same outcome they do not have to bargain. They need only make their preferences known. Not long ago, I drove my two youngest children to the video store to rent a tape. In the car they had a heated debate about whose turn it was to choose the movie. Unable to agree, they began to bargain. The older boy offered to let his brother pick the tape provided that he had the right to veto the younger's choice. Their negotiations turned out to be moot. After five minutes in the store, one of them found a movie they both had been eager to watch. The only sacrifice was dad's: Monty Python was not his cup of tea yet he was stuck with the bill.

Many business and political encounters are characterized by a high degree of consensus. The parties discover, if they did not know beforehand, that their preferences are remarkably similar. Pure consensus is nevertheless rare. There are almost inevitably small differences of opinion about the details of an agreement or its implementation. It may be necessary to bargain over these "loose ends." But if both parties are committed to the core of their agreement they are likely to have little difficulty in working out acceptable compromises about minor differences.

3. *The parties must have incomplete information about each other's preferences.* If either party knows its own and the other's preferences and all possible outcomes, it need not bargain. Choice is reduced to simple calculation. Real life situations are rarely so simple. One or both sides are often uncertain about the other's preferences or about the range of possible outcomes. The latter uncertainty is most likely when many issues are involved, or could be involved, raising the possibility of complicated trade-offs among them. A couple of years back, friends of mine rented a house for their sabbatical year in London. In the course of negotiating the price, they discovered that the English family had a dog they were reluctant to board and a teenage daughter who did not want to spend the year in Canada with them. They struck a deal and got the house at a reduced price plus the use of the family car in return for looking after the daughter and the dog.

Risk can generate further uncertainty. If both sides hold out for a more favorable settlement, agreement may be impossible, or unenforceable if it is reached. The Israeli-Palestinian negotiations illustrate these risks. In September 1993, Israel and the Palestine Liberation Organization (PLO) signed an agreement that envisaged Palestinian control of Jericho and the Gaza Strip as the first step toward a comprehensive peace settlement. Israel was to withdraw from these territories by April 1994, and Israeli and PLO negotiators were supposed to work out the details of the withdrawal by January. The negotiations dragged on for months as each side sought to extract the last pound of flesh from its longstanding adversary. The unexpected delay undercut the initial euphoria of the Palestinian and Israeli publics and gave time to the opponents of peace on both sides to mount campaigns of terrorism. In this changing political climate, analysts began to doubt whether any agreement, no matter how favorable, would be enforceable.

Yitzhak Rabin and Yasir Arafat pursued a high-risk strategy. Knowing just how much the other needed an agreement, each leader demanded concessions in return for timely acquiescence. The resulting stalemate threatened the entire peace process and was only resolved through the intervention of Egypt and the United States. In other situations risk can serve as a catalyst for agreement. People indicted for criminal acts routinely plea bargain and accept a judgment of guilt and a certain punishment to avoid the risk of greater punishment's arising from a conviction in a jury trial.

Bargaining can be considered a strategy for reducing uncertainty in situations of reciprocally contingent choice. Through the exchange of proposals, information, and threats, the parties attempt to provide or gain information about each other's preferences, expectations, and likely response to offers. Bargaining can go a long way toward reducing uncertainty, but as long as the three conditions listed here pertain, some need to outguess the other side will remain.

This view of bargaining as a strategy for reducing uncertainty requires us to distinguish between fact and certainty. One party's estimate of another's "bottom line" may be inaccurate, although the party making the estimate may feel confident about its judgment. Miscalculation can be the result of inadequate information, poor judgment, or "misinformation." In many bargaining encounters, parties find it strategically advantageous to mislead the other side about their preferences, resolve, or the nature of the constraints acting on them. By encouraging exaggerated estimates of these considerations, they hope to extract additional concessions.

Sometimes bargainers attempt to convey an accurate picture of their preferences, constraints, and willingness to entertain offers. They may do this because their preferences and constraints are largely transparent, or they fear the cost of having any bluff exposed, or they believe that a straightforward approach is more likely to result in a better agreement or postbargaining relationship. Later chapters examine these different approaches and the situations to which they are appropriate.

Our three conditions are necessary but insufficient for bargaining. Would-be bargainers may fail to recognize the extent to which their interests would be served by an agreement. When they do, they may be held back by powerful constraints. The leaders of Armenia and Azerbaijan have long been aware of the advantages of a negotiated settlement to their dispute over the territory of Nagorno-Karabakh, but they continue to fight a destructive war because they know that they cannot sell any accommodation to their compatriots nor enforce it in the absence of domestic support.

Bargaining begun in good faith between parties with strong common interests does not always lead to agreement. The 1992–93 Pittsburgh newspaper strike was costly to the newspapers—it put the *Pittsburgh Press,* its staff, and union employees out of business. But neither the newspaper owners nor the union was prepared to make the compromises necessary for agreement, despite their mutual recognition of how much they stood to gain from a settlement.

Bargaining can fail because one or both sides have no intention of reaching an agreement, although they may try very hard to convey the impression that they sincerely seek accommodation. "Phony bargaining" can placate important constituencies. The negotiations on conventional force reductions held in Vienna by the Conference on Security and Cooperation in Europe (CSCE) offer a classic example. In the 1970s, some of the smaller NATO countries were intent on cutting their military budgets. To forestall these cuts, the United States suggested that NATO negotiate mutual reductions with the Warsaw Pact. The Soviet Union agreed to negotiate for roughly the same reason, and, to the satisfaction of both superpowers, the talks dragged on for almost two decades without any significant progress. As long as the negotiations continued, Washington and Moscow pleaded successfully with their allies not to make any unilateral cuts in their defense budgets, as doing so would undercut their position at the bargaining table.

Phony bargaining can backfire. In the early 1980s, Margaret Thatcher's Conservative government had no intention of transferring sovereignty over the Falkland Islands to Argentina because the islanders wanted to remain British and had a lot of support in the British parliament. Thatcher was unwilling to tell Argentina about her decision, for fear of provoking a violent response. She attempted to finesse the problem through phony negotiations. British representatives held out the prospect of a transfer of sovereignty but never negotiated specifically about the issue. The Argentine junta caught on to Britain's ploy, walked out of the negotiations, and prepared for war in the hope of compelling the Thatcher government to enter into serious negotiations. The strategy failed and Argentine marines stormed ashore at Port Stanley on 2 April 1982.

To this point, most of my examples have involved only two sides. This is the simplest form of bargaining and most illustrative of its dynamics. Many bargaining encounters involve three or more parties; the Uruguay Round of the GATT negotiations had more than one hundred participants. Third parties who are not direct participants in the bargaining can also play a critical role, as the United States did in the negotiations between Egypt and Israel that led up to the Camp David Accords. President Carter employed a combination of threats and rewards to push the leaders of the two countries into negotiations and into making the concessions necessary for agreement.

Many two-sided bargaining encounters are more complex than they appear. In addition to bargaining with each other, one or both sides may need to placate important constituencies who may have the power to veto their agreement. The 1979 SALT II arms control accord, painstakingly negotiated with the Soviet Union, was submitted to the U.S. Senate for ratification as a treaty but was withdrawn by the Carter administration when it became apparent that the two-thirds majority necessary for approval could not be mobilized. Multilateral negotiations can suffer the same fate. In Canada, the 1988 Meech Lake Accord, which attempted to bring Quebec into the jurisdiction of the Canadian Constitution, was hammered out by the federal prime minister and the provincial premiers. It went down to defeat because of a filibuster waged by one native Canadian member of the Manitoba parliament that prompted the premier of New Brunswick, vehemently opposed to the accord, to withdraw it from his provincial parliament. A follow-on agreement fared no better. The 1992 Treaty of Maastricht on European economic integration was initially rejected by Danish voters and only narrowly approved in a French referendum. Widespread opposition caused European leaders to rethink their plans for further integration.

These examples indicate the critical importance of third parties. In many encounters, bargainers must negotiate simultaneously or sequentially with one another and with their respective constituencies. The principal bargainers may find themselves caught between the proverbial rock and a hard place. This usually puts them in a weak position, but as Chapter 10 shows, clever bargainers can sometimes derive a significant bargaining advantage from a dependent position.

Chapter 2

Why Bargain?

People, organizations, and states bargain because they want something someone else has or controls. To get it they offer something in return. Almost anything can become the object of bargaining. People routinely bargain about unpleasant chores at home or in the office, their salaries and benefits, and the price of goods they want to purchase. Organizations and governments bargain about everything from contracts to the scope of their authority; their bargaining is often conducted by professional negotiators.

The currency of bargaining is usually money, goods, or services. Any one or a combination of these may be exchanged for another. Typically, a bargainer offers something it values or needs less for something it values or needs more. A country that grows a surplus of coffee beans tries to exchange the beans it does not consume for oil, food, or manufactured goods, or for the money to purchase these and other commodities. For an agreement to be reached, the parties must agree on *what* is to be exchanged, the *ratio* of exchange, and the *scale* of the exchange. Colombia and Germany, for example, may agree to exchange coffee beans for credit in Deutsche marks, at a rate of 2.8 DM per kilo of beans, for a total sale of 10,000 kilograms of coffee beans.

Less tangible rewards can be sought or offered as payoffs. Secretary of State Henry Kissinger had the Federal Bureau of Investigation tap the telephone of his aide, Morton Halperin, to see if he was responsible for leaks to the press. Halperin found out about the tap, resigned in protest, and sued Kissinger for damages. The case was resolved years later when

Halperin dropped all charges in return for a public apology from Kissinger. In the negotiations leading up to the Camp David Peace Accords of 1977, Israel sought and received Egypt's recognition of its right to exist as a nation, symbolized in a peace treaty the two states would sign, in exchange for an Israeli withdrawal from the Sinai Peninsula. Both settlements were the result of intense bargaining.

People bargain to make gains and prevent losses. Marketplace activity is driven by the search for gain. Sellers of mangoes, computer chips, and pork belly futures aspire to make a profit by selling their product at a higher price than they paid to buy or produce it. In special circumstances, they may bargain to reduce losses. If merchants have stock they cannot keep or sell—spoiled mangoes are worthless—they may be willing, or even desperate, to sell at a loss to prevent even greater loss. Everybody knows that the best time to buy a car is after next year's models have reached the showrooms and dealers are anxious to sell the holdovers from the previous year that are fast losing their value. This principle is so well established that stores advertise liquidation sales in an attempt to attract customers on the lookout for bargains. I know a costume jewelry store in midtown Manhattan that has been going out of business successfully for over forty years.

Psychological experiments have indicated that people are generally more concerned to prevent loss than to make gains. They will take more risks to protect something they already have than to gain something new or additional. Parties bargaining to prevent or minimize loss are likely to respond in one of two quite different ways. They may be less willing to compromise than they would be if seeking gain, or they may be willing to grant major concessions in the hope of preventing further loss. Minimization of loss is why the U.S. government has been willing to sell property previously owned by failed savings and loans associations for a fraction of its estimated value.

Bargaining is not the only means of getting something somebody else has or controls, or of minimizing loss. Let us consider some alternatives:

Do without. If the price is too high, people may decide to do without, especially if what they seek is not essential. Economic or political considerations can prompt a decision to do without necessities. The Cuban economy was dependent on cheap Soviet oil. Following the collapse of the Soviet Union, the Castro regime decided to cut way back on oil consumption rather than spend scarce hard currency to buy oil at world market prices. In 1992, electricity, generated in oil burning plants, was severely rationed throughout most of the country, causing many factories to close.

Get it elsewhere. Products and services are often available from many sources. Buyers can and do shop around for the best price. Having lived in Italy, my family is addicted to bottled mineral water. My wife and I routinely drive across town to Pittsburgh's Strip District, where we have made a deal with a shop owner to sell Italian water to us by the case at a price that is less than half what we would pay in our local supermarket.

This strategy is less feasible in monopolistic markets. After the 1973 Middle East War, most oil importing countries had little choice in the short term but to pay the manyfold increase in prices set by the Organization of Petroleum Exporting Countries (OPEC). Fifteenth-century Venice, almost the sole supplier to Europe of imported Asian spices, was able to charge similarly high prices. The clamor for spice was an important reason behind Ferdinand and Isabella's decision to sponsor Columbus's expedition in search of a shorter, western route to India. They hoped to buy spices directly at the source and to capture Venice's profitable market.

Make it yourself. People handy with tools and having lots of spare time may be able to produce for themselves at considerable savings what they would otherwise have to purchase. Companies pursue a variant of this strategy when they begin to manufacture parts they previously bought from suppliers. Self-production can generate considerable savings for large businesses. At the national level this strategy is known as import substitution; leaders eager to reduce their country's dependence on other countries may invest in local production and try to protect fledgling industry through high tariffs. The United States did this with textiles in the early nineteenth century. In the latter half of the twentieth century, many Third World countries have pursued import substitution, with varying degrees of success.

Import substitution can also be used to improve one's bargaining position. In 1921–22, Mahatma Gandhi organized a boycott of British goods to put pressure on the government to grant self-rule. Across India, home-spun cloth was substituted for the products of Lancashire. The boycott did not lead immediately to home rule, but it did galvanize public opinion and support for the Indian National Congress.

Find a substitute. High prices encourage a search for alternatives. Before independence, Americans were tea drinkers. Following independence, the triangular trade pattern in the Atlantic was reversed, making it more profitable for Yankee merchants to import coffee from the Caribbean than tea from England. American drinking habits changed accordingly.

Inaccessibility also prompts a strategy of substitution. Castro's Cuba imported millions of bicycles from China to replace cars for which there was no longer any fuel. Wealthy industrialized countries may have open to them strategies that are similarly creative but more profitable. Britain, Germany, and the United States harnessed their chemical industries to develop wartime substitutes for dynamite, oil, rubber, and other critical products to which they were suddenly denied access. Development costs were high, but the strategy provided the governments with essential supplies in the short term and profitable new industries in the longer term.

Acquire through coercion. Throughout human history the strong have exploited the weak. Individuals, groups, and nations continue to use force, or the threat of force, to get what they cannot obtain by other means. In 1990, Iraq invaded Kuwait to gain control of that country's oil and gold reserves. A desperately broke but militarily powerful Saddam Hussein had previously tried and failed to convince Kuwaiti leaders to forgive some of Iraq's debt. He had also tried and failed to convince Kuwait and the United Arab Emirates to decrease their oil production in order to raise world prices.

Dispose of excess. Sometimes the problem is overabundance, not shortage, because the item in question cannot be sold at a good price, at any price, or otherwise eliminated. In years of bumper crops, farmers face this problem, and they have developed means for storing produce to sell it in the off season or in times of shortfall, when it will be in demand or fetch a higher price.

Currently, the biggest disposal problem in the United States is garbage. The cost and difficulty of garbage disposal has led businesses and municipalities to introduce recycling and biodegradable packaging and products. In the late 1980s, New York City confronted a garbage crisis when the federal government prohibited the dumping of waste in the Atlantic because it constituted a serious health and environmental hazard. New York City tried to find new landfills, but this proved expensive and at times embarrassing. For months, newspapers around the world carried the story of the infamous garbage barge loaded with New York's refuse steaming from port to port looking unsuccessfully for someplace to unload its despised cargo. In 1991, New York hit upon the clever idea of exporting organic waste, in the form of sludge, to western states for use as fertilizer. The farmers love the fertilizer and New York is saving millions of dollars that it would have spent on additional sewage facilities. City authorities are contemplating packaging the waste in pellet form and selling for a profit the sludge they were initially overjoyed to give away.

The choice between bargaining and some alternative strategy is further complicated by the need to consider the expected costs and gains of alternatives from short- and long-term perspectives. Strategies that are costly in the short term might be extremely profitable in the long term; this has often been the case with efforts to develop substitutes for expensive products and raw materials. Such endeavors require considerable funding up front but may pay handsome dividends if new, cheaper products come into use. Conversely, attractive short-term strategies can have disastrous longer-term consequences. The Reagan administration borrowed billions of dollars to finance large increases in military spending instead of raising the money through taxes. Today, the nation has a staggering national debt and high yearly interest payments, and the end of the Cold War and breakup of the Soviet Union rendered superfluous many of the weapons purchased in that costly strategy.

As the Reagan spending spree indicates, the choice between immediate and eventual effects often represents a choice between personal or institutional interests versus broader corporate or national interests. The Reagan administration chose to borrow and not to tax because taxes were—and always are—politically unpopular. Some future president would face the consequences of a mounting national debt. A similar calculation appears to have motivated the intense lobbying by the U.S. Navy to maintain twelve aircraft carriers although the Soviet Union had disappeared and most of its fleet was rotting in port.

Most if not all decisions between competing strategies and between short- and long-term interests turn on values. Social science offers little insight into how people and institutions frame these decisions and even less guidance about how they should frame them. Bargainers confronting complex situations of this kind need to ask themselves fundamental questions about their values and the short-term sacrifices they are willing and able to make for the sake of long-term interests.

So far, we have examined bargaining as an alternative to other strategies, but parties need not pursue bargaining as an exclusive strategy. They can simultaneously explore other avenues for advancing their interests.

In the 1980s, Frank Lorenzo, the owner of Eastern Airlines, entered into difficult negotiations with the unions representing the airline's employees. At the same time, he explored the alternative strategy of doing without, that is of selling the airline or putting it into Chapter 11 bankruptcy. Lorenzo's exploration of these options was well publicized, and he expected this to strengthen his hand with the unions. The unions mistrusted Lorenzo and held firm. His failure to reach agreement with them forced him to seek relief under Chapter 11 provisions, which resulted in big losses for him and for the airline's employees.

Soviet-American arms control negotiations offer an example of bargaining combined with coercion. Throughout the Cold War, arms control negotiations were accompanied by major efforts by the superpowers to develop or deploy the weapons any agreement might limit. This was a hedge against a breakdown in negotiations; neither side wanted to be at a disadvantage in an unconstrained strategic environment. It was also a ploy to gain "bargaining chips," weapons that could be given away in return for an equivalent or bigger concession by the other side. This logic was behind NATO's decision in 1979 to deploy a new generation of highly accurate nuclear-armed rockets and cruise missiles in Europe over the course of the following decade.

Getting it elsewhere is the most common alternate strategy pursued in conjunction with bargaining. While bargaining with one supplier, a company may simultaneously scout out other sources and more attractive terms. It may tell the first supplier what it is doing so it can play off one supplier against another in the hope of getting the best deal. This strategy is most effective when there are multiple sources and supply is greater than demand. Friends of ours recently parlayed an offer to their son of free tuition at a Big Ten school into a full scholarship that also provided for room and board, by threatening to send him to another prominent university that had offered a full scholarship.

The pursuit of multiple strategies can be a cost-effective means of coping with uncertainty; if bargaining fails, there is a ready alternative. Development of multiple options also puts pressure on the other party to be more accommodating. It is the sensible thing to do when there are doubts that bargaining will lead to a successful outcome.

Chapter 3

Is Bargaining Feasible?

The decision to bargain is based on the expectation that an acceptable agreement can be reached. This is sometimes apparent from the outset. The other side may have publicized its commitment to bargaining and its terms, or the terms may be dictated by known market conditions. The large volume and public nature of trading on the stock markets usually allow stock brokers to quote prices that are accurate within a quarter of a point.

Other bargaining situations are more problematic. When homeowners put their house on the market, it represents an intent to sell, not an irrevocable commitment. Even if offered their advertised price, which happens only in the most robust real estate markets, they may turn down the offer for any number of reasons. Prices usually reflect market conditions, and a knowledgeable buyer, or one with an experienced real estate agent, may have a good sense of what the property is worth and the range within which a settlement is likely. But people can be emotional and downright irrational about their homes or hold unrealistic impressions of their value. They may spurn offers that real estate agents and prospective buyers rightfully consider reasonable, even generous. A reasonable offer can also be rejected for perfectly rational reasons; someone may have submitted a higher bid.

When the feasibility of bargaining is unclear and the cost of bargaining failure low, it is reasonable to begin bargaining to learn more about the other side's interests and intent. Shoppers for used cars often find themselves in this situation. They can enter into negotiations with a seller and walk away if the vehicle is unacceptable or the price is not right. They can always respond to another advertisement.

Other bargaining failures are costly. Following the 1973 Middle East War, Egyptian president Anwar el-Sadat wanted to explore the possibility of an accommodation with Israel. A peace agreement could gain back the Suez Canal and Sinai Peninsula for Egypt, allow the government to cut its enormous military budget, and win American aid for economic development. Peace with Israel was anathema to radical Arab opinion, and any kind of overture to Israel was certain to arouse serious opposition at home and abroad. Also, Saudi Arabia could be expected to cut off the substantial aid it provided to Egypt. Unsuccessful negotiations were the worst possible outcome for Sadat. Egyptian and Israeli officials accordingly met secretly in Morocco to see if it would be possible to trade territory for peace. Sadat did not announce willingness to go to Jerusalem to address the Israeli parliament until he knew that Israeli prime minister Menachem Begin was interested in a peace treaty and would respond positively to his offer.

Estimates of feasibility are critical. If its initial soundings lead either side to conclude that an acceptable agreement is improbable, it will be unlikely to proceed further. This does not hold true for phony bargainers; they may be relieved to learn that an accord is unattainable. In the summer of 1914, when Austria decided to exploit the assassination of Archduke Franz Ferdinand as a pretext for war with Serbia, Austrian foreign minister Berchtold worked hard to produce an ultimatum that would with certainty be rejected by Serbian leaders. Even so, his wife reported, he spent a sleepless night for fear that Belgrade might accept the ultimatum just to expose his pretense. He breathed a sigh of relief when the Serbians balked at accepting the most humiliating conditions.

Off-the-table considerations can convince people to bargain even when they consider agreement unlikely or impossible. They may need to convince important constituencies of their interest in accommodation. Following the 1991 Gulf War, Israel and most of the Arab states agreed to attend the Middle East peace talks sponsored by the Bush administration. None of these countries really wanted to participate in the peace talks, but they nevertheless had to give the impression that they were committed to peace. They could not afford to antagonize the United States.

Negotiations are also a means of buying time. After their great victory over the Persian fleet at Salamis in 462 B.C., the Athenians returned home to their devastated city. Their first order of business was to reconstruct the walls around Athens and those that connected the city to its harbor at

Piraeus. The walls would make Athens invulnerable to assault or siege by land. Sparta, the most powerful Greek state of the time by virtue of its army, had commanded Athens not to rebuild its walls. Themistocles, the victor of Salamis, had his countrymen work around the clock on the walls while he went to Sparta to try to talk the Spartans out of their edict. Thermistocles dragged the discussions out until word arrived by messenger that the walls had been completed. He announced this *fait accompli* to the Spartans, who reluctantly recognized that there was nothing they could do about it.

Bargaining Goals

Estimates of feasibility presuppose that you know what you are bargaining for; without a precise objective it is impossible to assess the value of any outcome.

People sometimes have clear ideas about what is acceptable. Pensioners on tight budgets may calculate down to the penny how much they can spend on food. Both sides in a contract negotiation may come to the table with a clear understanding of their goals: the union may be willing to settle for nothing less than a wage increase equal to the rate of inflation, while management may be unprepared to grant an increase greater than the norm for the industry.

People are more likely to have thought more about their maximal objectives than their minimum conditions for agreement. The former can be gratifying, while the latter are more often anxiety arousing. If there are several issues at stake, they probably have not considered possible trade-offs among them. We are reluctant by nature to contemplate sacrifice until it becomes necessary, and even then it can be emotionally difficult, if not downright painful. An extreme version of the choice dilemma is explored in the movie *Sophie's Choice*. A Jewish mother during the Holocaust has the opportunity to save one of her two children, but she is unable to choose between them and both perish.

In organizations and governments, officials are often reluctant to consider bargaining trade-offs for more practical reasons. A decision to bargain may require painstaking efforts to put together a coalition of powerful individuals who need to be convinced that an accord will benefit their personal or institutional interests. Coalitions are often fragile and based on diverse and possibly competing interests. Leaders may accordingly have a strong incentive to avoid any discussion of possible concessions.

They may reason that concessions, inevitably at the expense of some component of their coalition, will be easier to sell when an agreement has taken shape, a broad array of interests support it, and the cost of opposing it is correspondingly greater. Henry Kissinger kept South Vietnamese president Nguyen Van Thieu completely in the dark about the substance of his Paris peace talks until he had reached an agreement. Kissinger then presented Thieu with a *fait accompli* rejection of which would alienate the American Congress.

Bargainers sometimes fail to consider trade-offs because of inexperience, shortage of time, or lack of imagination. Shortly after his inauguration, President Bill Clinton promised to do away with discrimination against homosexuals in the armed services. His announcement provoked widespread opposition within the military and on relevant congressional committees. Unwilling to ride roughshod over this opposition, the president negotiated a compromise arrangement with the military. By doing so, he antagonized the military, who did not want any homosexuals in their ranks, and the gay community, whose hopes for a total reversal in military policy he had earlier encouraged.

Carl von Clausewitz urged leaders never to take the first step before considering the last. His advice, meant for princes contemplating war, is equally applicable to bargainers. Failure to think through one's interests and derive bargaining preferences from them, or to think about the interests of the other side and the preferences they are likely to dictate, can result in superficial and faulty estimates of the feasibility of bargaining. A faulty estimate can deter a party from bargaining when that action is in its interest, or can encourage it to bargain when doing so is not. The former leads people to adopt alternative strategies that may be costly and not serve their interests as well. The latter can result in fruitless negotiations that waste time and resources and may antagonize constituencies who were opposed to bargaining or committed to its successful outcome. People who commit themselves to bargaining may set in motion a process that ends up forcing them to accept an accord they are unhappy with and do not consider in their interest.

On-the-table versus Off-the-table Issues

The meaning of any bargaining encounter is determined by its context. For those intent on squeezing the last bit of advantage from the other side, on-the-table issues are critical. For those concerned with how the outcome will affect other important interests, off-the-table issues will dominate.

On-the-table versus Off-the-table Objectives

When the best deal is the primary objective:	*When clinching the deal is the primary objective:*
On-the-table stakes are high.	Off-the-table stakes are high and dictate agreement.
The bargaining is iterative and the outcome will set a precedent for subsequent negotiations.	The terms of the agreement are unlikely to set any precedents.
The outcome will influence other negotiations.	There are no reputational concerns.
The bargainer's reputation is at stake.	It is important to establish or maintain a relationship.
There is little concern for establishing or maintaining a relationship.	

As a rule, parties will be interested in getting the best on-the-table deal when the stakes are high, when the bargaining encounter is a one-time affair, when they have no interest in building or maintaining a relationship with the other party, or when they believe their bargaining reputation is on the line. The prospective buyer of a used car, who is making a major purchase and never expects to see the seller again, is likely to try to pay the lowest possible price for the car.

Parties will be willing to settle for less when the stakes are low, when other more important issues hinge on a successful outcome, when the encounter is iterative, when the relationship is important, or when their bargaining reputation is not at stake. An entrepreneur, hoping to generate more business for his or her company, may be willing to offer a much lower price than usual to clinch the sale. A friend of mine recently went into business as a commercial landscape architect. She was eager to make her reputation and thrilled when a major corporation asked her if she would be interested in designing the grounds around their new corporate headquarters in Pittsburgh. The commission the company offered her was almost beside the point; she bargained instead for more money to be allocated to the cost of the landscaping, so she could do the kind of job that would attract a lot of attention and help her get subsequent, lucrative contracts with other large companies.

This is not an isolated example. Major commercial transactions are also influenced by off-the-table considerations. The Japanese buy most of

Jamaica's premium Blue Mountain coffee crop. In recent years, this coffee has become much sought after in Germany and France, and in 1992 European buyers offered the Jamaicans higher prices to obtain more of the coffee. Jamaican coffee growers rejected the European offers and continued to sell most of their produce to the Japanese for lower prices.

The Jamaican decision to sell coffee to Japan for less than the world market price was entirely rational. Japan had provided extensive aid to coffee growers when their fields had been devastated by a hurricane. The Japanese could be counted on again, to provide aid if natural disaster struck or to contribute in some other way to the coffee industry's well-being. Jamaican coffee growers were willing to sacrifice the short-term gain of selling Blue Mountain beans to European buyers at higher prices in favor of the long-term benefits they expected from the Japanese. Jamaican coffee growers were investing in a relationship.

Not every bargaining decision is motivated by instrumental calculations. People sometimes value relationships for their own sake. In the movie, *The Shootist*, John Wayne plays an elderly gunslinger dying of cancer. In a poignant scene, he sells his beloved horse to the owner of the local stable. The two men bargain fiercely over the price and end up agreeing on the sum of $300, very close to the gunslinger's original asking price. The stable owner opens his roll top desk to get the cash but discovers he is five dollars short. The gunslinger insists on the full amount. The buyer takes five gold coins from one of the drawers in the desk and places them one by one in John Wayne's outstretched hand. "Two ninety-six, two ninety-seven," he says, but is stopped short before reaching two ninety-eight. "That's enough," says our hero, "you keep the rest." The stable owner's face breaks into a smile, and he exclaims, "So I am the best bargainer in the world!" "Yessiree," drawls Wayne, as the two men shake hands. For the gunfighter about to die, a warm personal encounter was more meaningful than a few extra dollars he would never have the opportunity to spend.

In these three examples, off-the-table considerations were reinforcing. In other bargaining encounters, they are crosscutting. People can be pulled in opposite directions by conflicting off-the-table concerns or by conflicts between on- and off-the-table considerations.

The classic example of conflicting on- and off-the-table considerations is the chief operating officer who recognizes that a reorganization or merger agreement is in the best interest of the company but who confronts a board of directors adamantly opposed because it will limit their power and perquisites. The CEO may be forced to choose between the interests of the company and his career. In the infamous RJR Nabisco takeover, the CEO clearly put his personal interests first, arranging a multimillion-dollar personal settlement at the stockholders' expense.

Recognition, evaluation, and choice among competing on- and off-the-table considerations can be the most difficult aspect of bargaining. These tasks become especially challenging when they must be carried out in a fluid and unpredictable environment. President Jimmy Carter's ill-fated attempt to negotiate a strategic arms limitation treaty with the Soviet Union illustrates this problem.

Carter was deeply committed to strategic arms control because he believed that it would significantly reduce the risk of nuclear war. When he came to power in 1977, he inherited the outlines of an arms control treaty that had been hammered out the year before in Vladivostok by Secretary of State Henry Kissinger and Soviet Premier Leonid Brezhnev. Carter was dissatisfied with this accord because it did not require either superpower to make deep cuts in their strategic arsenals. He antagonized Moscow and the American military by insisting on renegotiation. Arms negotiations are a painfully slow process, and in the course of what became known as the SALT II talks, domestic support for arms control waned as détente with the Soviet Union became more problematic. Carter persevered and reached an agreement in 1980 but withdrew the proposed treaty from the Senate following the Soviet invasion of Afghanistan. He judged correctly that it would have gone down to defeat.

At the beginning of his presidency, Carter did not see any contradiction between the national interest and his political interest. By late 1978, as opposition to SALT grew, Carter was being pulled in opposite directions but remained committed to the national interest, as he interpreted it. When it became clear that the prospective treaty would not receive the required two-thirds vote, Carter became increasingly anti-Soviet in his public pronouncements and tried, without success, to recoup the domestic political support he had lost by his earlier sponsorship of arms control.

The Carter example indicates how well-informed and intelligent people can get into trouble when they misjudge their interests or the constraints acting on them. Carter erred by spurning the Vladivostok accords. By insisting on deeper cuts, which required lengthy negotiation, he delayed an agreement by several years. By the time the new agreement reached the Senate, the political climate had changed dramatically and had become unfavorable to arms control. Carter's laudable attempt to get a better deal on the table resulted in no deal, because of off-the-table constraints.

Fortunately, most negotiations are less complex than SALT and less subject to the vagaries of the political or economic environment. But, as the next chapter shows, they can still require choices about what is important and what, if anything, you are prepared to give up. Only then, can you determine whether bargaining is feasible.

Chapter 4

From Theory to Practice

The preceding chapters analyzed prebargaining: the process by which you decide whether you want to bargain, what you want to bargain for, and whether bargaining is feasible. The analysis stressed the overriding importance of interests in determining the answers to all three questions.

Interests have little meaning in the abstract. Everybody wants security, health, and happiness for themselves and their loved ones. This tells you little about how they will act in specific situations. Interests take concrete shape and inform behavior only when people contemplate choices that entail sacrifice. When you may be forced to give up something of value to preserve or obtain something else of value, you need to assess the relative importance of what is at stake. You need to consult your interests.

The movie *Sophie's Choice* shows how some trade-offs can be too painful to consider. A colleague recently faced this problem in a much less dramatic way. A prominent Ivy League university asked if he would be interested in a well-endowed chair. The prospect was appealing; the chair would provide funds for his research and make his closest collaborators his new colleagues. But there would be costs for his family. His wife had only recently found a terrific job after years of unsatisfactory part-time employment, their oldest child was in her second year of high school and very attached to friends she had known since childhood, and it would cost a lot to buy a home in the new city. The more he thought about it, the more my friend came to believe that a move was impractical and that any attempt to explore the possibility would create an immediate crisis for his family. It was better not to express interest in the position and to say nothing to his wife.

Sophie's Choice was about the prevention of catastrophic loss. If Sophie had been able to choose between her children, one of them might have survived. My professor friend, in contrast, was offered the opportunity to make attractive but marginal gains. In declining any interest in a chair he could not accept, he passed up the possibility of using a job offer to extract more salary or research support from his home institution.

Bargaining for gains is a voluntary opportunity. If the prospect arouses anxiety because of the possible trade-offs it would entail, you probably should give it a miss. My professor friend acted wisely in declining to pursue marginal gains that would have created anguish for his family, but also for himself. He explained that to land the chair he would have had to sound convincing about his commitment to relocate, and to do that he would have had to convince himself how much better off he would be with a chair and close proximity to his collaborators. This would have made it more difficult for him to turn down the chair if it had been offered, and he would have been unhappy after doing so.

Bargaining to avoid loss is a more serious matter. Sophie and her children paid an enormous price for her inability to make a choice. As a general rule, you should make your best effort to face up to emotionally difficult trade-offs when there is a lot at stake, because of the cost of not doing so. The short-term gain of anxiety and conflict avoidance rarely compensates for long-term substantive losses. In our society, the prototypical example of counterproductive conflict avoidance is husbands or wives who stay in a bad marriage. Afraid or reluctant to confront their spouse or to accept the emotional turmoil, economic costs, and social embarrassment of a separation, they convince themselves that all will work out. Several years and several children later they feel utterly trapped, because the costs of breaking up are now so much greater. They may regret not having acted more decisively when they first realized their marriage was on the rocks.

This chapter explores both kinds of bargaining situations. It walks the reader through a family decision to buy a new car and a mayor's attempt to keep a professional baseball team from relocating. Both cases were framed as problems of loss avoidance, but opportunity also entered in. More importantly, both cases illustrate how the three steps of prebargaining are applied in practice.

To Buy or Not to Buy

In October 1994 my family faced an unpleasant problem. We had two aging cars but inadequate resources to replace either without drawing on money put aside for college tuition. Our 1984 Honda Accord had a rusted frame and strained to maintain its speed on the slightest upgrade; our boys had nicknamed it "The Little Engine that Could." Its operational radius extended no farther than the airport, and my wife felt that that was pushing it. Our 1986 Honda Civic also had some rust, from its years in Ithaca, where salt was used very freely on the roads. It was more reliable but increasingly uncomfortable for our two strapping teenage boys and unusable as a family car when their older sister came for a visit.

The Alternatives

We had tried to postpone the day of reckoning as long as possible. We had opted for the strategy of doing without. We had both cars inspected and serviced regularly, put a new clutch in the Accord and new brakes in the Civic, and renewed our AAA membership to ensure emergency road service. On the few long trips we took as a family we rented a large car at a reasonable weekly rate. Repair and rental costs were much less than the costs of replacement. But the repair bill went up every year and the cars, especially the '84 Accord, became less reliable. There was also the question of safety; neither vehicle had air bags or antilock brakes. We felt increasingly uncomfortable about driving our children around in rattletraps. My wife and I had several long discussions about our needs and the best way to satisfy them. We came to the reluctant conclusion that we could no longer go on as before; we had to replace the '84 Accord. We looked at the alternatives: a new car, a late model used car, and leasing. None of them seemed attractive. A new car, bought or leased, would cost a lot of money. A used car would cost less but would not have dual air bags and would cost more to maintain. The most attractive solution—selling both cars, moving to Paris, and relying on public transportation—was alas, out of the question.

The unappealing prospect of shelling out thousands of dollars for a car, used or new, encouraged us to think again about keeping the Accord one more year. But another trip to the airport brought us back to reality; we had to bite the bullet and replace the car. The other catalyst for our decision was the arrival of financial aid forms from the several universities to which my elder son was applying. In looking over the forms it immediately became apparent that any liquid assets we declared would automatically be credited to tuition. If Eli received a scholarship, the less money we had the more he would get. We had already put some money away to help defray the cost of his education. The additional $17,000 we had in the money market suddenly constituted a problem. We had to spend or hide it, and hiding it would be dishonest. The obvious solution was to buy a car.

The only problem that remained was what to do if Eli did not get an additional scholarship to top off what he would receive from his National Merit scholarship and my employer. If we spent all or part of the $17,000 in the bank on a car, we would need to borrow money from somewhere. Two possibilities emerged: a student loan and a loan from my father-in-law. The latter would be interest free, and the former would be at a low interest rate with no repayment until graduation. With commercial interest rates on the rise, family or university loan had appeal.

Putting all this information together, Carol and I decided to shop around for a new car. It was a more attractive proposition than a used car that would cost less—leaving us money in the money market—and not be equipped with dual air bags. Leasing would also require less of a cash outlay and cost more in the long term. One other consideration pushed us toward new cars: the possibility of getting a good price on a 1994 model that was still on the lot and costing the dealer money to keep. If we could not find a suitable and attractive '94 or get a reasonable deal on a 1995, we could still look into leasing and used cars.

Bargaining Goals

Carol and I began to talk about the kind of car we wanted. We had some fairly definite requirements: a four-door sedan with dual air bags, antilock brakes, air conditioning, comfortable and easily adjustable driver's seat for a tall husband and short wife with vulnerable backs, and rear seats with enough legroom for teenagers. We also wanted a Japanese car. We had rented American cars and did not like them. They were unresponsive to steer, unobtainable with manual transmission, difficult to drive in snow with their archaic rear-wheel drive, and seemed to come equipped with seats designed by chiropractors hungry for business. Two of the last three I had driven through rain storms had dripped all over me when I opened the driver's door. Japanese cars had none of these faults, and were cheaper than their European competitors because many of them were assembled or even produced in the United States. So we would start with Honda, but also check out Toyota, Mazda, and Nissan.

Like every shopper, we wanted the best product at the cheapest price. To get a better understanding of quality and cost, we read *Consumer Reports* and other relevant literature, spoke to a friend who was a car expert, and consulted friends who had recently purchased Japanese cars. We learned that all four brands were highly regarded by analysts and owners alike. Almost everybody advised against the luxury cars these manufacturers produced (the Acura, Lexus, Maxima), saying they were very expensive and loaded with unnecessary options. We did not have that kind of money in any case. We decided we should look instead at Accords, Camrys, 626s and Altimas, all of which came in LX models that would have everything we needed. The consensus among our friends was that we would get a trade-in of between $500 and $1,500 on our '84 Accord and have to pay somewhere in the range of $17,000 for an Accord, Camry, or 626, and less for the smaller Altima. With the initial bargaining goal of trying to beat this estimate, we set out to make the rounds of dealers.

Feasibility

We went first to the Honda dealer, where we were well known to the service manager. He introduced us to the salesman. We told him what we were looking for and he described four '94 Accords on the lot, two of which met our specifications. Carol, our younger son David, and I had a close look at them and tried out the seats, front and back, while we listened to the usual pitch about the Accord's sterling features and warranty. The salesman promised "to work with us" to come up with a good deal. After examining our '84, punching buttons on his calculator and scribbling with his pencil, he came up with the figure of $18,300, and that included the trade-in. We thanked him politely and drove down the street to the Mazda showroom.

The Mazda salesman had a lot full of '94s but had difficulty finding a 626 with a stick shift. Mazda buyers apparently prefer automatics. He finally located a car, but it turned out to be a top of the line 626 with a larger, 2.5-liter six-cylinder engine, leather seats, and most of the bells and whistles found on luxury cars. Its list price was almost $23,000. I told him that we could not afford such a car but would like to check out its seats and see how it compared with the standard 626. It was very comfortable, and had the advantage of multidirectional electronic controls. Back in the showroom, the salesman tried without success to interest us in a '94 automatic or '95 manual. I made it clear that I liked the car I had sat in but did not need all of its extras and was unwilling to pay the "rock bottom" $19,500 he was asking for it. The salesman wanted to know how much I would pay. No more than $17,000, I told him; this is what I had budgeted for a car. "Out of the question," he insisted.

We made one more stop that day, at Mercedes-Nissan. We walked into a showroom filled with posh Mercedes and amused ourselves by checking out a couple of price tags. At least one of the cars cost more than would my son's entire college education. A salesman approached and asked if we would like to look at a Nissan. The patch in my jeans must have given me away.

They had no '94s with manual transmissions but promised to "work with us" (here we go again) to come up with a good deal on a brand new '95. We inspected a new Altima and took it for a road test. It handled well but was too cramped in the back for the boys. I asked if anyone had ever crashed a car on a test drive. No, the salesman said, but a couple of teenagers had come very close. He assured us that he was going to get the lowest price possible from his boss and disappeared into his office. He came out with an offer of $16,000. We thanked him and left.

On Monday, all three salesmen called to ask if we had bought a car. When I said no, each immediately offered a substantial discount on the price he had quoted on Saturday. This encouraged us to persevere in the hope of getting a good deal.

Analysis

Alternatives

Carol and I relied on a series of questions to identify our interests, their relative importance, and their implications for any decision about cars. We asked ourselves the nature of our problem, the extent to which we were responding to a need or opportunity, the various ways of addressing our problem, and their advantages and drawbacks. The list of alternatives developed in Chapter 2 helped us structure this inquiry and kept us from imposing too narrow a frame of reference on the problem. In the course of working through the alternatives, we realized how complex a decision we faced. There were several different ways we could address our transportation needs; it was not simply a choice of a new car or continuing with the status quo. We also discovered that we could not evaluate these alternatives without considering a second problem: our elder son's college education. The solution to the car problem turned out to require some prior choices about the tuition problem.

Our effort to identify our interests indicates the extent to which real world problems are ill defined and tend to merge into one another. This is a blessing and a curse. The complexity makes defining interests and evaluating alternatives more difficult, but it can facilitate problem solving when it increases the alternatives and the trade-offs they permit.

Our car experience further indicates that bargaining opportunities may not be driven solely by need or opportunity, but can be determined by a mixture of both. Our car purchase was need driven: we had to replace an increasingly unreliable and unsafe vehicle. However, our decision to shop for a new car was also motivated by opportunity: October was a good time to hunt for bargains because dealers needed to unload '94 models still on their lots. Our decision was the result of a push and a pull. To our surprise, the relative weight of these motives changed after we visited the showrooms.

Our choice also reflected our preferences. An American car, say a Ford Taurus, would have met our needs just as well as a Japanese car. It would come equipped with air bags, antilock brakes, and air conditioning and might be a little cheaper. However, it would not satisfy our preferences: we would have to settle for an automatic transmission and all the drawbacks we associated with American cars. For these reasons, we never considered an American car, although this option would still be open to us if we failed to find an appropriate Japanese car at the right price.

Bargaining Goals

Having specified our interests, we used them to set bargaining goals. Our interests dictated two kinds of goals: one concerning the nature of the car, the other the price we were prepared to pay for it.

Our car requirements were straightforward. Our cost requirements were a response to competing considerations. We had a real price constraint; any outlay beyond what we had in the money market would force us to draw on other assets or income that we would need for Eli's college expenses. But we also needed to clear out the bank account so we would not show savings on a college financial application form. These competing concerns dictated an optimal expenditure of $17,000 and the need to pay for the car in cash.

There are occasions when interest dictates spending more rather than less. People who sell houses and need to put the profit into another house or pay taxes on it face this situation. So do foundations who are required by law to give away a certain percentage of their yearly income to retain their tax-exempt status. The larger lesson illustrated by this aspect of prebargaining is the need to break free of rigid and often superficial conceptions of goals and to think about your interests and what will serve them best.

In reaching our bargaining goals, we consulted the list of on- and off-the-table objectives displayed in Chapter 3. It became immediately apparent that our interest was in getting the best on-the-table deal. The outcome of the negotiations had no implications for any other negotiation, our reputations were not at stake, nor were we interested in building a relationship.

Feasibility

Estimates of feasibility are different from determinations of interests and bargaining goals, because they require considering the problem from the perspective of the other side. That requires insight into the other side's interests. Bargaining is feasible when there is some overlap in the range of outcomes acceptable to both sides.

Estimating the cost of cars, new and used, is relatively easy. The value of used cars can be determined from the *Blue Book,* which gives the value ranges for all models over a period of years. Manufacturers make no secret about the list price of new cars, and dealers routinely advertise discounts. Dealers' prices, almost always below list, represent the opening bid in a bargaining game. The real question is how much below that price they are willing to go. *Consumer Reports* and other publications provide useful information about dealer pricing and discounts.

We had reason to surmise that all of our dealers could be coaxed into making major concessions: they needed to make way for the new year's models, the value of the older cars was decreasing every month they sat unsold, and some dealers have to pay a monthly fee to the manufacturer for every car on their lot.

Our expectations were confirmed by several events. Two of the dealers had recently run big ads in the papers offering handsome discounts on last year's models. Three of the four dealers had offered additional discounts on the spot. All four subsequently called to offer further reductions.

Our estimates of feasibility were greatly facilitated by the existence of multiple suppliers. Each dealer was eager to provide information about the other to justify his price. From the Honda dealer, who was unwilling to offer as big an initial discount as his neighbor at Mazda, we learned that Mazda was having trouble moving its cars and had offered dealers a $3500 rebate for any '94s they sold. That explained why the Mazda 626 we had looked at was marked down from $23,000 to $19,500. The Mazda dealer claimed that he was selling at cost but we now knew better. The Nissan dealer told us how much a month it cost Toyota and Mazda to keep cars on their lots.

Our initial round of visits to dealers was a successful research exercise. We gained the information we needed to determine the feasibility of paying something in the range of $17,000 for the kind of car we wanted. We came away encouraged that this was not only possible but that through clever bargaining we might do even better. Information is power.

Feedback

I have portrayed our prebargaining about a new car as a linear process. Determination of interests set bargaining goals that in turn allowed us to explore the feasibility of bargaining. In practice, prebargaining often functions like a feedback loop. The process of setting bargaining goals can stimulate second thoughts about one's interests, and the exploration of feasibility can encourage rethinking of bargaining goals or interests. Our car experience is a case in point.

Our efforts to test the feasibility of our bargaining goals led us to reformulate those goals and, to a lesser degree, our interests. It was quite likely that we could buy the kind of car we wanted for the price we were willing to pay. But an unexpected opportunity had presented itself: a more powerful, luxurious Mazda 626 with very comfortable leather seats that we might be able to pick up for the same price as the standard, underpowered Accord or Camry. We knew the car was something of an anomaly—a top of the line sedan with a stick shift—and therefore difficult to sell. Thanks to the Nissan salesman, we also knew how much the Mazda dealer had to pay every month to keep it on the lot.

The motive of opportunity suddenly entered into the bargaining picture. Carol and I decided to bargain with the Mazda dealer to see if we could buy his more attractive car for $17,000. If we failed, we lost nothing. We could still negotiate with the Honda and Toyota dealers over less luxurious models. Time was on our side. If we waited another month, we might get a better deal.

The change in our bargaining goals compelled us to rethink our interests. The possibility of getting a more expensive car for the same price seemed very attractive at first blush. Everybody likes a bargain. But we really needed to consider the pros and cons of this particular bargain. The advantages were obvious. It was more powerful and comfortable, had a nice feel of solidity, and came equipped with an antitheft system, electric moon roof, and better sound system. There was also the intangible but important psychological feeling that I would get something special in return for my $17,000, and that would make the expenditure more palatable. There was also drawbacks. Pittsburgh had an extraordinarily high incidence of auto theft because it was the closest major metropolitan area to the chop shops in the hollows of West Virginia. The more expensive the car, the more attractive it became to thieves. A six-cylinder 2.5-liter engine also uses more gas than the four-cylinder, 1.75- or 2.0-liter engines on the standard models. Indulgence won out, and we began to plan our strategy for getting the Mazda dealer to lop another $2,500 off his price.

Play Ball?

The second case of bargaining is about the offer by a consortium of local businessmen to keep a professional baseball team in a midsize American city in return for a new stadium, to be built and financed by the city. The consortium portrayed their offer as a great opportunity for the people of the city; it would keep their beloved, if not so successful, ball team in town, along with all the business revenue it generated. Some members of the city council disagreed. In their view, a new stadium would be expensive, and its putative economic payoffs would benefit a narrow, wealthy business elite. Both sides looked to the mayor for support.

The situation was complex from every perspective. The current owners, a very wealthy family, were the *bêtes noires* of the city's sportswriters and fans. For the sake of short-term profit, they had sold off some of the best players, denuding the team of much of its talent. Five years earlier the team had won a pennant; for the last two years it had been at the bottom of its division. The All Star selection committee had been hard pressed to find a single player, which the rules required they must, for inclusion on the league's team. By contrast, one of their pitchers had won the Cy Young Award the year after he was sold, and a former outfielder had led the league in hitting and runs batted in. With the team's fall to the cellar, attendance had declined and with it, revenues.

Two years before, the current owners had threatened to move the team to a burgeoning Sun Belt metropolis unless the city agreed to build them a new stadium. The public had been outraged, and the mayor and city council had refused to discuss the proposal. The owners had applied to the league for permission to relocate but had also let it be known that they were willing to sell their franchise for a reasonable price. A consortium of local investors had stepped in and negotiated an eighteen-month option to buy the team for an agreed-upon price.

The consortium's option was worthwhile only if the city could be coaxed into building a new stadium. The current stadium was decrepit and had woefully inadequate parking. A new, attractive, and accessible ballpark would draw more fans and generate more revenue. One economist estimated that baseball could become a "cash cow" for the city. The consortium made it clear to the press that they would use any extra revenue to build a better team. A more successful team, especially a pennant contender, would draw more fans and generate more revenue. The team could ultimately become a successful investment. If the city refused to build the stadium, the consortium would have to let its option lapse and the current owners would probably get league approval to move the franchise.

The consortium was hopeful that the city would respond positively. Its members were prominent citizens who had served on the boards of local charities and community organizations and had done a lot for the city. They waged a largely successful media blitz that stressed their concern to keep the team in town and the importance of the team for the economy and self-esteem of the city. They insisted that they were prepared to make the city a fair offer from which everybody stood to gain. So far, they had received favorable press.

From the mayor's perspective, the consortium represented a terrific opportunity. When the possibility of the team's leaving had first arisen, he had asked a local public policy school to study the economic consequences for the city. It was reported that they would be considerable. Paid attendance the previous year had been 750,000, and more than half of those people had come from outside the city, mostly from the suburbs. The city had earned $315,000 in taxes on the $4.5 million box office take. About half the taxes went to pay for police and other ballpark-related services. Fans had pumped another $78 million into the local economy through their expenditures on refreshments, parking, hotels, restaurants, and shopping. In addition to these measurable economic benefits, the city would lose whatever standing a professional ball team conferred, making it more difficult to attract new businesses.

To keep the team, the mayor would have to reach an understanding with the consortium. He would then have to bring it before the city council for approval and ask them to authorize a bond issue to pay for a new stadium. The voters would then have to pass on the bond issue. The mayor had two negotiations to conduct: one with the consortium and the other with a possibly recalcitrant city council. He had to offer attractive enough terms to the consortium to make it worthwhile for them to exercise their option to purchase the team, but not give them so much that the city council rejected the deal. Without the active support of most of the city council, he would have difficulty in selling the bond issue to the electorate.

For the mayor, the best outcome was an agreement acceptable to the consortium, the city council, and the voters. The worst outcome was failure to reach agreement with either the consortium or the council. The baseball team would leave the city and the mayor's opponents would blame the loss on him and make it an election issue. It would be better not to raise the hopes of the city's sports fans unless he could strike a bargain that the city council would approve. The feasibility of agreement was a paramount concern.

The mayor told me that the more he thought about his interests the more he came to believe that they required doing whatever was necessary to keep the team in town. He had no preferences about the terms of the deal; he would support any arrangement that was acceptable to the consortium and the city council. The problem was to find common ground. Although the consortium was composed of civic-minded people who had done a lot for the city, they were first and foremost businessmen, who expected their investment to be profitable. The eleven-member city council was a diverse body. All of its members had the best interests of the city at heart, but they could rarely agree about the substance of those interests. Most of them wanted to keep the ball team in town but would almost certainly oppose any deal that gave the appearance of rewarding rich investors at the city's expense.

To build a consensus, the mayor needed to know the range of outcomes acceptable to the consortium and the city council. This would be difficult to ascertain. Neither side was about to reveal its bottom line, and it was doubtful that the city council even had any idea about what its bottom line was. It was more likely that one or both parties would table unrealistic demands, in the expectation that they could be traded away for meaningful concessions. The mayor could sound out the consortium and city council, and the former would almost certainly submit a proposal, but he would still have to make an educated guess about what either was prepared to settle for.

The consortium spoke with one voice; the five investors were long-standing friends and seasoned businessmen. They knew the value of giving at least the appearance of unanimity. They had selected one of their number, a particularly experienced negotiator, to represent them. The mayor would never have any doubts about the consortium's position, but it would be difficult for him to penetrate their veil and learn more about their minimum conditions.

The city council presented a different problem. Its eleven members represented diverse constituencies and did not work well together. The council could not be expected to formulate its own position; rather, it would react to any proposal presented to it by the consortium or the mayor. The mayor could count on two of its members to support him through thick and thin; they were his associates and had ridden into office on his coattails. They would provide him feedback on the thinking of other members of the council, to the extent that members made their views known. The other nine members, although all Democrats like the mayor, were independent. One of them had mayoral ambitions of her own and could be expected to say and do whatever was likely to garner her favorable publicity. The council's loose identity would make it difficult to work with, but its lack of unity would enable the mayor to deal with its members individually. Perhaps he could build a majority coalition in favor of accommodation with the consortium.

The mayor realized that the outcome of any negotiation would be influenced by how it was structured. There were many possibilities. He could bargain with the consortium and subsequently present whatever agreement he reached to the city council for their approval. He could talk to the council first, describe the issues that were likely to come up in negotiations with the consortium, and then proceed on the basis of their instructions. Other possibilities were to negotiate with both groups at the same time or to involve representatives of the council in his negotiations with the consortium. Each approach had distinct advantages and drawbacks. The mayor immediately ruled out the possibility of going before the council first; at least one of its members was almost certain to set conditions that would be impossible but nevertheless appealing to the public, and then put herself in a position to criticize the mayor for getting anything less from the consortium. It would be better to go to the consortium first, even though the mayor would not know beforehand the kind of agreement the council would be likely to accept. Upon reflection, the mayor decided that his best bet was to learn the general outlines of the deal the consortium envisaged and then to consult informally with some of the undecided but more reasonable members of the council to elicit their reaction and suggestions. He would then decide whether it was feasible to proceed. If it was, he would keep council members informed about the progress of the negotiations and, if possible, secure their provisional approval for the parts of any package that emerged.

From the mayor's perspective this strategy had distinct advantages. It would provide him with information from the outset about the consortium's goals and some council members responses. Before proceeding to negotiate he would know something about the most likely areas of disagreement that needed to be bridged and perhaps what might be done toward this end. He could also use the feedback he got from council members to coax concessions from the consortium, on the grounds that it was necessary to get council support for the bond issue.

Analysis

Alternatives

The ball team case is very different from the car purchase case. In thinking about buying a new car, the biggest challenge my wife and I faced was thinking through our interests. We had several interests at stake, and some of them appeared to be in conflict. We also had several alternatives to consider, and each of them involved complicated trade-offs. The mayor's interests were crystal clear from the outset. He wanted to keep the ball team in town, and an arrangement with the consortium appeared to be the only way to do this. There were no alternatives to consider. A deal with the existing owners or attracting a new team to the city were out of the question.

Our search for a car was unambiguously need based, as was the mayor's commitment to keep professional baseball alive in his city. He nevertheless regarded the consortium's interest in buying the team as a golden opportunity, just as we viewed the possibility of acquiring a more luxurious Mazda for the same price as a normal sedan as an opportunity not to pass up. Carol and I saw eye to eye on the car, but the mayor and members of the city council did not agree about the ball team. Council members differed about whether a proposal from the consortium would represent an opportunity or a cost for the city. For at least one member of the council, who had previously announced his opposition to any city support for a privately owned sports team, it would be a breach of public trust and a waste of scarce resources to try to bail out a failing business. Other council members would make up their minds in response to the particulars of the deal; most of them were undecided and perhaps open to persuasion.

The baseball case highlights the subjective nature of interests and how the assessment of what constitutes an opportunity or a cost is determined by the frame of reference that is brought to a problem. For the mayor, the economic well-being of the city and his own political interests were lenses through which he viewed the problem. He understandably regarded the consortium as an opportunity. The antagonistic council member was first and foremost committed to keeping public debt to a minimum and therefore saw any bond issue as a cost and all the more intolerable if public money was going to help a small group of investors make a profit.

In considering interests, bargainers will inevitably rely on some frame of reference to organize the problem. That frame of reference is likely to determine which interests are considered paramount and, by extension, what the bargaining goals will be. Had Carol and I framed our car problem as a transportation problem to be solved with as little expenditure as possible, we might have decided to lease or to buy a cheaper, American car. A different mayor might have structured the baseball problem differently; his predecessor had adamantly refused to consider building a new stadium, because it would have rewarded the owners at the city's expense. His decision had prompted the owners' decision to seek a new home.

People sometimes make bad decisions because they use inappropriate frames of reference. They use the first frame of reference that comes to mind, one that worked in another deceptively similar problem or one suggested to them by someone who does not share or understand their interests. People also use inappropriate frames of reference when they fail to think about their implications. The city council member committed to lowering the public debt opposed any bond issue because he believed that debt was contrary to the city's interest. His approach could also be criticized as an overly narrow and rigid formulation of the public interest. Debt may allow a city to do something to the long-term benefit of its citizens that it could not pay for out of current income. The city's airport, which facilitated its growth as a regional hub, is a case in point. It brought revenue and jobs and additional income that more than pays the debt service. The mayor contends that a new ballpark could do the same.

In the process of analyzing your interests in a bargaining situation, ask yourself why you have chosen a particular frame of reference. Are there other frames of reference you might consider? What implications would they have for your determination of interests? Are they more or less appropriate? Why is this so? Working through this checklist of questions will not inevitably lead you to the best frame of reference, but it will help. It will sensitize you to the possibility of choice, the importance of that choice, and the need to justify to yourself whatever frame of reference you choose.

Bargaining Goals

In buying a car, we set twin goals concerning the characteristics of the car and its price. Both goals were shaped by many considerations. With our bargaining goals established we sought to establish their feasibility by making the rounds of car dealers. For the mayor, the process was the reverse. His objective was agreement, any agreement that would pass muster with the city council and be approved by the voters. Feasibility was decisive. It would determine whether the mayor would bargain, what he would bargain for, and with whom he would bargain.

Feasibility

It was relatively easy for us to determine the feasibility of our bargaining objectives. Automobile dealers advertise their prices, and consumer advocacy groups publish information about dealer markups and price structuring. After a little research and a few visits to showrooms, we had a very good idea about the kinds of '94 cars that were available and what we would have to pay for them. We also had several dealers with whom we could do business just in our part of the city. This choice significantly increased our chances of finding the kind of bargain for which we were looking.

For the mayor, feasibility was not only his major concern but his major problem. He had three constituencies to satisfy: the consortium, the city council, and the voters. At the outset, he knew little about the preferences or bottom lines of any of them. The city council was especially unpredictable because of the divergent interests of its members. The mayor also knew little about what could be done to bridge the gaps that might emerge in any negotiations.

There was also a difference in cost. Carol and I could change our bargaining objective if our attempt to purchase the Mazda 626 for $17,000 proved unsuccessful. We could shop for a different car or even decide to look into the possibility of a lease or the purchase of a used car. The mayor had no such choices. The consortium was the only game in town, and unsuccessful negotiations with them would hand a big political stick to his opponents to beat him over the head with in the next election. An arrangement with the consortium that the city council rejected and opponents characterized as a sweetheart deal for the mayor's friends would leave him equally exposed.

Another important difference concerned events over which neither the mayor, the consortium, nor the city council had any control. Beyond its antiquated stadium, the greatest financial drawback the franchise faced was the challenge of being a small-market team. The loss of its industrial base had caused the city to shrink in size, making it among the smallest metropolitan areas to support professional sports teams. The team not only drew fewer fans but received proportionately less from cable and television rights. The owners were hard pressed to pay competitive salaries, which in recent years had become astronomical.

Revenue sharing or salary caps would help ameliorate this situation, but a proposal to this effect had provoked the 1994 baseball strike. The mayor, facing the prospect of negotiations before that strike was resolved, had no idea of the extent to which any settlement would provide relief for small-market teams. The Major League Players Association had proposed a tax on revenues and leaguewide sharing of revenues on broadcast deals made by individual clubs. Arrangements of this kind were already in effect in the American League. Revenue sharing and standardized accounting procedures could prove a financial windfall for the local team. Another unknown in this case was the additional revenue that a new ballpark would generate. Camden Yards in Baltimore and Jacobs Field in Cleveland had proved that intimate, urban ballparks with grass fields, easy access, and fine amenities could draw huge crowds. A *Financial World* analyst estimated that skyboxes, luxury suites, and in-park advertising could boost revenues by an additional 20 percent and that even more revenue could be generated with the addition of a hotel, shops, restaurants, and offices. The city could recoup much of its outlay through rent and taxes on these subsidiary operations. But to build this kind of complex, the city would need support from the state and the Regional Development Authority (RDA). This would require additional negotiations, with the governor and leaders of the legislature.

Adding revenue sharing and a ballpark complex to the picture would greatly facilitate the mayor's task. He could offer fewer concessions to the new owners and have a more attractive proposal to present to the city council. Unfortunately, he would have to begin negotiating before he knew anything for certain about revenue sharing or state and commercial support for a new stadium. In August 1994, when the mayor had to make his decision whether or not to entertain a proposal from the consortium, there was no end in sight to the players' strike, and any arrangement with the state and the RDA would take a lot of time to work out.

Finally, there was the problem of ratification. Any arrangement acceptable to the consortium and city council would entail a bond issue that would require approval by the voters at the next election. Nobody knew how the electorate would respond or what new issues might arise between the negotiations and the elections which might shape public reaction to a bond issue. Presumably, whatever arrangement was worked out would also build on the expectation of some kind of league support for the team in the form of revenue sharing and state and RDA support for the city and its new stadium. As these arrangements could not be worked out beforehand, the deal with the consortium would have to be contingent on them.

The Decision

Faced with this enormous uncertainty, the mayor compared his plight to a blindfolded swimmer on a high diving board about to execute a half gainer without knowing if there was any water in the pool below. The mayor got as much information as he could before making his decision to jump. He spoke informally to members of the consortium and coaxed from them the general outlines of the kind of proposal they would submit. He sounded out local businesses on their willingness to coinvest with the city in the stadium and its associated hotel, restaurants, and shops. A major hotel chain had expressed enthusiasm. The mayor also had several discussions with the governor and key city delegates to the state assembly. The governor was encouraging but could not promise anything. The local press, which had learned of a possible deal from a source on the city council, was also favorably disposed.

The mayor spent a long weekend trying to calculate the odds of putting together a successful deal. They were impossible to compute. The prospect of revenue sharing, a stadium complex, state and RDA aid, and local investment made the effort attractive but unpredictable. Any or all of these pieces of the puzzle could fail to fall into place. He really had no way of knowing. In the end, his decision reflected his personality. He welcomed challenges, and that's what tipped the scale. "What the hell," he told his administrative assistant the following Monday morning, "let's play ball."

Prebargaining Checklist

This chapter has used two different cases to illustrate the common steps of prebargaining and the challenges they can entail. The car purchase decision was an everyday problem, a variant of which most readers have undoubtedly confronted. It turned out to be complicated but relatively easy to resolve. The baseball decision was complex from the outset because of the number of parties involved, the uncertainties surrounding the finances of the baseball team, the kind of stadium the city would seek to build, and where and whether it could raise and borrow enough money for the complex. In shopping for a car, we were able to set precise bargaining goals and determine their feasibility before proceeding. The mayor was unable to do either but was still compelled by his interests to proceed.

The principals in both cases went through a similar process to determine their interests, bargaining goals, and the feasibility of bargaining. Based on these cases and the information in the preceding chapters, I have developed a checklist for these critical steps of prebargaining. Not all of the questions are relevant to every bargaining problem. You need to identify and answer those germane to your situation.

Interests

1. *What is the problem?* Is it need based or opportunity driven? If both components are present, which is dominant?
2. *What frame of reference have you used* to define the problem and

determine whether it is need based or opportunity driven? Are there alternative frames of reference you could use? Would they lead to different understandings of the problem? What are the relative merits of these competing frames of reference? Which best represents your interests?

3. *Does your problem provoke anxiety?* What are the causes of that anxiety (e.g., uncertainty, risk, the apparent lack of any good solutions, the need to make difficult trade-offs, having to deal with people who are unpleasant or with whom you have a strained relationship)? What can be done to reduce the anxiety (i.e., can you address any of its sources)? If the problem is need based, what can you do to cope with the remaining anxiety? If opportunity based, would you be better off not to bargain?

4. *Is your problem linked to other problems?* Will the solution to your problem require solutions to other problems? If you resolve your problem, will it be easier or more difficult to solve other problems? Do your answers to these questions encourage you to reassess the nature of your problem or the extent to which it represents a need versus an opportunity?

5. *Make a list of your interests* affected by the problem. Try to rank them, to give you a clearer idea of what is essential as opposed to desirable. If you cannot rank them, at least divide them into two categories: essential and less essential interests.

6. *What alternatives are open* to you to protect or advance these interests? Work through the list in Chapter 2 (do without, get it elsewhere, make it yourself, find a substitute). Assess the short- and long-term advantages and drawbacks of each of the applicable alternatives. Given your interests, what course of action is most attractive (or least repugnant). If it entails bargaining, proceed to the next stage of the process.

Goals

7. *What objectives do you seek?* Bargaining rarely has one goal. How many do you have? You should consult your list of interests to formulate your responses.

8. *Rank your bargaining goals.* To do this, you need to know which of your goals are need driven as opposed to preference driven and which

of the former are most important to you. Here too, you should consult your list of interests for guidance.

9. *What is your bottom line?* In bargaining there is almost always a tension between efforts to attain maximal goals and to achieve agreement. In most bargaining encounters, you need to give something up to get an agreement. It is best to consider beforehand what goals you are willing to compromise or trade away for the sake of agreement. What is essential? What are you willing to do without? Your ranking of bargaining goals should help you answer this question.

10. *How important is an agreement?* This depends on your interests. You need to assess them horizontally and vertically. You have already defined the problem, your interests that are affected, and the bargaining goals they dictate. You also need to consider, if you have not already, how the bargaining encounter will influence future bargaining encounters and important relationships. Consult the list of on- and off-the-table objectives in Chapter 3. It constitutes a checklist to help you determine the relative importance of the terms of an agreement versus the agreement itself.

11. *Double check your alternatives.* Assume for the sake of argument that you will have to settle for your bottom line. If so, is an agreement still more attractive than other alternatives open to you? If not, should you consider exploring one or more of these alternatives before you bargain or in tandem with bargaining? If agreement becomes necessary and there are no alternatives or no good alternatives, you might want to reconsider your bottom line. Would you still be better off with an agreement even if you had to concede more? Conversely, if you have more attractive alternatives, you should consider raising your bottom line.

Feasibility

12. *How costly is bargaining?* If it does not involve major expense or commitment of time or put your reputation on the line, you have little to lose and perhaps much to gain from bargaining. When the costs of bargaining, or bargaining failure, are high, feasibility estimates are critical. In this circumstance, you need to work through items 12 through 15 in this checklist. You do not want to bargain until you have a reasonable idea of the prospects for agreement.

13. *Estimate the other side's bargaining goals.* In some bargaining encounters this is a simple matter. The other party may have publicized its goals, they may be dictated by well-known market conditions or easily inferred from its past behavior. In other bargaining encounters this may require extensive effort, as it did for the mayor trying to fathom what kind of agreement would be acceptable to both the consortium and the city council.

When information about the other side's preferences is unavailable, you can try to make educated guesses. Try to put yourself in the other side's shoes and identify the frame reference it is likely to bring to the problem. What definition of interests will this frame of reference lead to? What bargaining goals will these interests dictate? Do the other side's actions and statements provide any insight into these questions?

14. *Compare the range of outcomes* acceptable to both (or all) sides to determine the feasibility of bargaining. The greater the overlap, the more likely the prospects of agreement.

15. *What is the impact of third parties?* In some bargaining encounters agreement depends on the response of third parties. Our mayor needed state funding and commercial commitments to put together the kind of package he could sell to the consortium and city council. Would your agreement be hostage to third parties? Is there anything you can do beforehand to predict or influence their behavior or reduce your (or the other side's) dependency on them? To answer the last question, you may need to learn more about the third party's interests and preferences.

Putting It Together

If bargaining is your best alternative and you have set your bargaining goals and they seem feasible, you can proceed. You have satisfied the three conditions of prebargaining. But any one of these conditions can prove problematic. Let's look at what you can do in such circumstances.

If choosing the best of your alternatives is the problem it is usually because of uncertainties associated with one or more of them. If there are nonbargaining alternatives, it may be possible to explore them before bargaining or simultaneously with bargaining. You can try to draw out the bargaining to gain time for learning more about the other alternatives. If you begin bargaining, you may also learn more about the shape of any agreement that is likely to emerge. The additional information may help you discriminate more effectively between or among alternatives.

Difficulty in setting bargaining goals is usually a reflection of other problems. The most common of these has to do with the definition and ranking of interests. You cannot establish bargaining goals unless you know what you want and what you are prepared to sacrifice to get it. If this is the problem, you need to go back to items 5, 7, 8, and 9, and work them through more definitively.

Attempts to set bargaining goals can also be confounded by difficulty in assessing the appeal of other alternatives or the power balance between the parties. Uncertainty about either consideration makes it hard to know how much you can reasonably expect to get from the other side or how much you will have to concede to get an agreement. The problem of alternatives is dealt with above, and that of the power balance in Chapter 8.

Feasibility can be difficult to establish because the other side's preferences are opaque or the responses of critical third parties are unpredictable. If exploratory bargaining is cost free, you can proceed to bargain and see how things develop. If the kind of agreement you seek appears unattainable, you can walk away from the negotiations. If bargaining entails real costs but nothing critical is at stake, you can spurn it at the outset.

Problems arise when something important is at stake, the costs of bargaining or bargaining failure are high, and the outcome of negotiations is unpredictable. You must make a difficult decision on the basis of incomplete or uncertain information.

There may be some way to finesse this decision. You should explore the possibility of informal, exploratory, or even secret talks to get more information about the other side's intentions and bargaining goals. If the omens are good, the prospect of public bargaining may appear more attractive. Henry Kissinger and Chinese foreign minister Chou En-lai met secretly in Pakistan to work out the broad outlines of an accommodation before Nixon was officially invited to Peking. The Egyptians and Israelis held secret talks in Morocco to discuss the possibility of Israel's returning the Sinai in exchange for a peace treaty before Sadat announced his willingness to go to Jerusalem. Israel and the Palestine Liberation Organization held extensive talks under cover in Norway to work out their accommodation. Those discussions were initially between private individuals who could easily be disowned if the talks failed or became public knowledge. When progress appeared feasible, increasingly senior officials took part.

If exploratory talks, back-channel communication, or secret negotiations are out of the question or inconclusive, your dilemma remains. Before making a decision, you should make another attempt to think through the relative merits of negotiation versus non-negotiation. Make a list of all possible costs and gains associated with both options. If the costs outweigh the rewards, proceed no further. If the rewards are greater, go on to consider the likelihood of successful negotiations. You need to weigh the expected benefits of success against the probability of failure. This is very difficult to do. Like the mayor, your decision in the end may turn on your intuition and attitude toward risk taking.

Part 2 Strategies of Bargaining

Chapter 5

How to Choose a Strategy

You are ready to bargain. You have identified your interests, established your bargaining goals, and estimated their feasibility. Now you need to choose a bargaining strategy. This chapter is intended to help you make that choice. It describes three different strategies of bargaining and the situations to which they apply. The strategies themselves are analyzed in detail in chapters that follow.

Gaps versus Surplus

When you framed your bargaining goals, you thought about the minimum terms that would make an accommodation worthwhile. This is your bottom line. You also thought about what else you would like to achieve in the negotiation.

It is absolutely essential to have a well-defined bottom line. This is the minimal objective and the benchmark against which to measure all offers and counteroffers. Sometimes the bottom line is need driven. You may simply not be able to afford to pay more than $7,000 for a car. On other occasions, the bottom line may reflect preferences. You really do not want to spend more than a certain amount on renovations. It is not worth it to you, given what else you could do with your money. Either way, the bottom line represents the condition(s) needed to make accommodation worthwhile or attractive.

It is just as important to have a clear idea about other objectives. If shopping for a used car, you may be reconciled to paying the Blue Book price of $8,000 for the model in question (your bottom line) but still hope to pay closer to $7,000 for a car in good condition with relatively low mileage and in your favorite color. If you are adding a deck and patio to your home, you may be prepared to accept a bid of $10,000 but also hope to get the contractor to pass on his discount on materials and accept a penalty if the job is not complete by a given date. The lower price for the car and the extra conditions for both the car and the renovations represent your maximum goals.

The other side can be expected to approach bargaining in much the same way. It will be committed to satisfying at least its minimum conditions, but like you it will hope to obtain more. Accommodation is possible if the two sides can find an outcome that satisfies their respective bottom lines. Sometimes, there is considerable overlap in their preferences, presenting them with many possible outcomes. Framing the problem in this way makes it apparent that there are two fundamentally different kinds of bargaining encounters.

In Type I bargaining encounters, no agreement seems possible at first because no outcome can be found that satisfies the minimum conditions of the sides. The challenge is to find some way of bridging the gap between them. Suppose our mayor from the last chapter elicits from the consortium a list of the conditions they think they must meet to make purchase of the baseball franchise profitable. If one or more of those conditions require a financial commitment from the city that the city council refuses to authorize, there is no basis for a deal. The mayor must get the consortium or the city council or both parties to reconsider their positions, or frame some other proposal both will find acceptable.

In Type II bargaining encounters, more than one agreement is possible. There is a zone of agreement, in which the preferences of the sides overlap. At least several and perhaps many agreements would satisfy their minimum conditions. The problem is to decide who should satisfy which additional preferences.

Type II bargaining is often a two-step process. The sides first feel each other out to see if an agreement is possible. Once they discover that cooperation is mutually advantageous, their efforts shift to claiming as much of the surplus as possible. This stage of the bargaining may be quite conflictual.

The goals you established in prebargaining were provisional. They reflected your interests and expectations of what was possible to obtain. As you begin to bargain, you may not learn anything new about your inter-

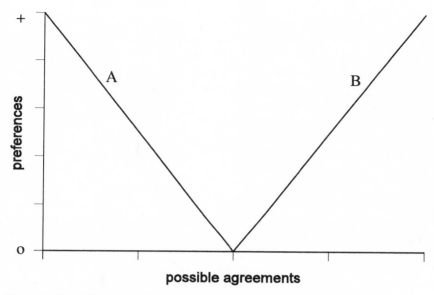

Figure 1. Type I Bargaining Encounters

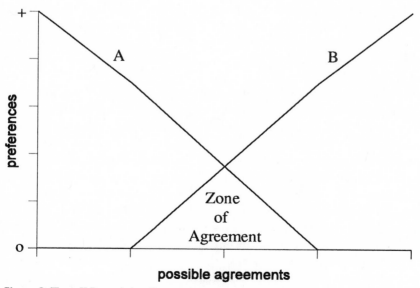

Figure 2. Type II Bargaining Encounters

ests, but you are almost certain to learn more about the kind of agreement that is possible. Fairly early on in the bargaining, it should become apparent what kind of bargaining encounter you confront. If it is a Type I encounter, you (and the other side) probably need to lower your expectations. It is even possible that one or both of you (better it should be the other side) may have to relax your bottom line to get an agreement. In Type II encounters, your bottom line is not at issue. Depending on your initial expectations, you may be able to make an upward revision in your bargaining goals.

Strategies

In Type I encounters, your goal is to bring about an agreement that does not require sacrifice of bottom line goals. In Type II encounters, you want to secure a percentage of the surplus. Chapters 6 through 8 analyze three bargaining strategies suitable to these goals. The *strategy of coordination,* the subject of Chapter 6, treats bargaining as a cooperative exercise. It requires participants to exchange information about their preferences and to use that information to search for the most satisfactory accommodation. The *strategy of rewards,* addressed in Chapter 7, attempts to make an outcome acceptable by making it more attractive. The *strategy of punishment* tries to compel acceptance of the terms by making rejection too costly. Toward this end, it employs threats of nonsettlement and punishment. In common with the strategy of rewards, it attempts to manipulate the other side's estimates of the costs and gains it would incur by accepting or rejecting of the offered terms.

The strategy of rewards is most appropriate to Type I bargaining encounters, where the sides must find some way of bridging the gap between them. That gap is the result of conflicting interests. The strategy of rewards addresses this problem in three different ways. It relies on low-cost concessions, side-payments, linkage, and other tactics to reward concessions or reduce their perceived cost. If this fails to bridge the gap, it tries to expand the scope of bargaining by introducing new issues of interest to the other side. By doing so, it attempts to cobble together an accommodation that is acceptable to the other side, although individual components of it may not be. If necessary, the strategy encourages the other side to reframe the bargaining problem and reconsider the implications of different outcomes for its interests. A new frame of reference can lead to a shift in preferences that makes agreement possible.

The strategy of coordination is most commonly used in Type II encounters, where the problem is the distribution of surplus value. Bargainers exchange information about their preferences and work together to find a solution that satisfies those preferences as much as possible. They also cooperate to find mutually acceptable ways of overcoming whatever gap remains between this solution and the preferences of the sides. The strategy works best in situations where the preferences of the sides are largely compatible.

The strategy of punishment can be used in Type I or Type II bargaining encounters. In the former, it uses threats of punishment to compel the other side to lower its bottom line and settle for less. In the latter, it relies primarily on threats of nonsettlement to convince the other side to settle for fewer gains.

It is important to bear in mind that Type II encounters are fundamentally cooperative in nature. Both sides recognize that a zone of agreement exists and that they will be better off with an agreement than without one. They accordingly have a strong incentive to reach an amicable agreement about the surplus. If coordination fails, leaves some issues unresolved, or is not applicable in the situation, one or both sides are likely to invoke shared principles to justify their claims. Only if this fails should you consider threats that exploit a favorable power balance. Coercion is a strategy of last resort in Type II encounters and usually attempts to bring about only minor shifts in the target actor's preferences.

Caveats

The fit between bargaining strategies and bargaining encounters is not so neat in reality. The three strategies are best suited for the purposes we have described, but any of the three, depending on the circumstances, can be used with either kind of encounter. They can also be used alone, in combination with other strategies, or in sequence. Chapters 6 through 8 examine these complexities and develop a set of guidelines to help you make the necessary choices.

Our cursory overview of bargaining indicates that the essential step is to determine what kind of bargaining encounter you confront. Type I and II encounters pose different problems and generally require different strategies. The nature of some bargaining situations may be obvious. It may quickly become apparent, for example, that the other side has financial or other constraints that make it very difficult for it to meet your bottom line. Alternatively, you may be haggling with a distributor over the price of a hot product, and both of you expect to reap fat profits regardless of whether you accept each other's terms.

At times, it is not easy to distinguish Type I from Type II encounters. You may not know where the break-even point is for the other side and whether your offer represents a loss or a profit. The other side may also try to mislead you by falsely portraying its bottom line. It may gain a lot from convincing you that a Type II encounter is really a Type I. You may demand less or be more willing to make concessions if you think it is necessary to procure an agreement. In many situations, you need additional information to judge with any certainty what kind of encounter you face. You may even need to reject the other side's terms to see if it is bluffing. This aspect of bargaining is also treated in the succeeding chapters.

Whatever strategy you choose, keep in mind that bargaining consists of contending and problem solving. When preferences largely overlap and you rely on the strategy of coordination, you engage in problem solving. But the ensuing struggle over any surplus or gap can be very contentious. The strategy of rewards, which seeks to resolve differences by expanding the win set, also emphasizes problem solving. But these differences emerge only in the course of contention. When preferences are further apart, you may need to rely on the more contentious strategy of punishment. But threats to walk away from the table succeed only when the other side believes that an agreement would be in its interest. Threats work best within a broader context of problem solving.

Chapter 6

The Strategy of Coordination

The strategy of coordination attempts to treat a bargaining encounter as a cooperative exercise. It is appropriate to situations in which an agreement can be constructed that closely approximates the preferred outcomes of the two or more sides. The strategy requires participants to exchange information about their preferences and to use that information to search for the most satisfactory accommodation.

Only weeks before writing this chapter, I had recourse to the strategy of coordination in negotiations with my dean over the directorship of our graduate program in international affairs. He wanted me to take over the program, and I was reluctant to do so because additional administrative responsibilities would cut into my research time. I knew I was facing a losing battle; one by one my colleagues had made it known to the dean during the course of the semester that I was their candidate for the job.

In March, the dean called me in for a talk about the directorship. I acknowledged the need for a senior professor to run the program and agreed that other senior faculty had already served or were unacceptable for one reason or another. I indicated my willingness to assume the directorship if some way could be found to protect my research time. The dean asked what I had in mind, and I suggested a two-course reduction in my teaching load and more administrative and secretarial support. He promised to see what he could do.

The dean and I had clashing preferences. He wanted me to be director, and I did not want the job. If I took the position, I wanted something in return, and the dean, facing an across-the-board budget cut from the university, wanted to conserve his fast-dwindling resources. We also had strong overlapping interests; both of us wanted a prominent and well-run international affairs program. By providing detailed information about my preferences, I gave the dean the opportunity to transform our bargaining encounter into a collaborative game. He responded by using this information to put together an offer that maximized, as far as possible, the interests of both of us.

The strategy of coordination is appropriate only in special circumstances.

A mutually satisfactory solution must exist. There must be sufficient overlap in the preferences of the parties for them to be able to find a solution they are happy with. My dean came up with a one-course reduction in teaching, additional secretarial assistance, an assistant director, and a modest salary increment. He met almost all of my conditions at little cost to himself.

The issues must be linked and have asymmetrical utilities. When there are many issues on the table that can be combined in many different ways, it is sometimes easier to construct an outcome that rewards all sides. Agreement is even more likely if some of these issues have asymmetrical utilities. If the benefit of receiving a concession is greater than the cost of making it, the principal demands of one or both sides may be met at little cost to the other.

My negotiations with the dean touched on four different issues: salary, teaching, and secretarial and administrative support. The latter two of these issues had strongly asymmetrical utilities. The value to me of having a graduate student to do much of the "grunt work" was enormous. It cost the dean next to nothing. He had already awarded a number of assistantships to needy students and had to find faculty or staff for whom they could work. The secretarial staff were on contract and it would not cost the school any more money to give me more of their time.

The asymmetries in my negotiation were weighted in the right direction: the value of receiving concessions was high, and the cost of making them low. When the reverse is true, asymmetrical utilities impede or prevent agreement. People are understandably reluctant to make concessions they perceive to be costly. This is why the dean initially refused my request for a two-course teaching reduction. He explained that other program directors, who now received a one-course reduction, would demand a second course off, and this the school could not afford.

There is a third condition, which is helpful but not essential to collaborative bargaining: *Mutual trust must exist between or among the parties.* I was only willing to reveal my preferences to the dean because I trusted him and knew that he was keen on finding some way to convince me to accept the directorship.

Successful use of the strategy of coordination does not always require a high degree of trust between the parties. When the stakes are high and the prospect good that coordination will succeed, even bitter adversaries may attempt to cooperate. In August 1939, Stalin and Hitler took the world by surprise when they announced their nonaggression pact. These seemingly bitter foes had also struck a secret deal to invade Poland and divide it between them. More recently, Croatia and Serbia, who had just fought a war with each other, worked out an arrangement to dismember and divide Bosnia. Croatia subsequently cooperated with Bosnia in military operations against Serbian forces.

The Mechanics of Coordination

The strategy of coordination requires each side to know something about the other's preferences. Such information can be learned through the formal exchange of offers and counteroffers, both of which serve as conveyor belts for information about preferences. With any luck, the exchange of offers and counteroffers allows the parties to zero in on the best deal, but with many issues and many possible trade-offs among them, the exchange can sometimes be very hit or miss in its results. It is more efficient to exchange information about preferences directly.

The dean and I used a combination of the two approaches. I volunteered information about my preferences, the dean then made offers to which I reacted. By providing information about my preferences at our first discussion, I made the dean's task easier. My comments and answers to his questions made it clear that I valued compensation in the form of free time more highly than a salary increment. This confidence provided the basis for the arrangement we ultimately worked out. The dean was more reticent about his preferences. This imbalance in information was appropriate to the situation; the dean was more vulnerable to exploitation if his preferences became public knowledge.

The strategy of coordination is often a two-stage process. The initial stage is characterized by coordination: the two sides search for an accommodation that maximizes their respective interests. If they find one, it is still likely to fall short of their preferred outcomes. In my negotiations, the gap concerned teaching and the dean's reluctance to break with precedent and offer me two courses off in return for assuming the directorship.

In the second stage, the residuals issues are addressed. There are a number of ways parties can deal with them. One or both sides can agree to make a sacrifice, they can split the difference, or one side can persuade the other to make a concession. New issues can also be introduced to reward the side making a concession. To overcome our gap, the dean and I both made concessions. I offered to forgo half the salary increment he had offered if he agreed to a two-course reduction. To help him cope with the equity problem, I came up with statistics that showed that International Affairs had twice the faculty and students of any other program in the school and thus required twice the effort to manage. The dean then objected to giving me a two-course reduction because everyone else who could teach the introductory theory course would be on leave. I offered to teach the course and to bank the credit for a course off to use some other year when it did not create a problem. We struck a deal. The dean even threw in a sweetener: he would excuse me from service on the time-consuming doctoral admissions committee.

Problems and Solutions

The strategy of coordination can fail at any stage. Parties can exchange information about their preferences but not come up with any arrangement that meets their respective needs. They may then resort to the strategies of punishment or reward to try to bring about an accommodation. The Uruguay round of the GATT talks is a case in point. After the successful conclusion of the Tokyo round, member countries began with high expectations; they hoped to move quickly to further reductions of tariff and nontariff barriers. Early efforts to collaborate revealed significant differences among the participants over agricultural tariffs and intellectual property. While they bickered, domestic agricultural lobbies mobilized, making agreement even more difficult, and prompting a shift in the negotiations from coordination to hard-nosed bargaining that relied on threats of nonsettlement and retaliation.

Problems can arise even after a possible accommodation has been found. The parties involved may be unable to bridge the gap between that accommodation and their preferred outcomes. To attain their goals, one or both sides may use harsh words or threats that undercut their earlier efforts at coordination. Last year, the in-laws of a close friend died within six months of each other. The four children thought it would be a relatively straightforward matter to divide the estate. Their parents' wills were up-to-date and apportioned their financial assets equally among the children. Their mother had drawn up a list assigning household effects, pictures, and memorabilia to members of the family who had expressed interest in them. All of the children had been sent copies of the list. Warren, a lawyer and the only child still living in the family's hometown of Providence, had been appointed executor. He arranged for his three siblings to join him over a weekend to sort out and dispose of their parents' personal effects.

The family reunion started out well. The children and their spouses, three of whom were present, reminisced about their childhood and shared warm memories of their parents. The trouble began when Warren passed out copies of his mother's list. Melanie, the senior sibling, was upset that Susan, her younger sister, was to get the family Bible, which she maintained had been promised to her. Susan reminded her that some years before they had reached an agreement: she would get the Bible and Melanie the silverware. They had all previously seen the list, why had she waited until now to raise an objection? Warren's suggestion that his mother's collection of European pewter be given to a museum and the children divide the resulting charitable deduction triggered another dispute. His brother Jonathan and his wife wanted the collection and offered to compensate the other siblings for it. They were flabbergasted by Warren's valuation of the collection at $18,000. They insisted it was worth no more than $8,000. This angered Melanie; Jonathan's undervaluation of the pewter, she complained, was unfair to the rest of them, whose tax deductions would be significantly reduced.

The reunion ended on an acrimonious note. Melanie and Susan reached an accommodation about the Bible and the silver, but the question of the pewter continued to divide the family. Melanie and Jonathan exchanged some harsh words, and Warren's attempt to mediate their dispute was rudely brushed off by Jonathan, who accused his older brother of being overbearing and manipulative. A subsequent independent valuation of the pewter failed to resolve the dispute and only created more ill-will. The core settlement, about the equitable distribution of financial assets, began to unravel. A disagreement arose about how much of the loan Jonathan had received from his father to start his business he had paid back. A year later, nothing has been resolved, and Warren has threatened to take his brother to court.

The family dispute is only superficially about objects and money. It is really about relationships. This also happens in business and international relations where off-the-table issues in the form of past wrongs, unresolved rivalries, and personal or group antagonisms often dominate bargaining and prevent agreements between parties with obvious common interests in reaching agreement. Even when a core agreement is reached, disputes over residual issues can poison relationships and destroy what looked like a done deal.

In dealing with residual issues, the importance of what is at stake and the nature of the relationship between the parties usually dictate the strategy. When residual issues are not critical and the relationship is important, parties will be reluctant to make threats, even if threats might pry concessions loose from the other side. No-holds-barred bargaining is destructive to relationships. The dean and I treated each other with kid gloves because maintaining our good personal and professional relationship was more important than anything either of us could possibly gain by hanging tough in this encounter. When there is no relationship to preserve, neither party may have any qualms about shifting from coordination to conflict.

The strategy of coordination is also sometimes used after the strategies of punishment and rewards have failed. Not long ago, my wife mediated the divorce settlement of a couple who had been sparring through their attorneys for over a year. At his counsel's suggestion, the husband had cleaned out all the joint accounts and had hidden other assets to make them inaccessible to his wife or the courts. The wife had retaliated by rejecting her husband's request for joint custody and had made it difficult for him to visit with their children. Common sense finally prevailed. Under pressure from another couple with whom they were both still close, they began to talk about the kind of settlement each of them envisaged and discovered that their expectations were not that far apart. Three sessions with a mediator led to a comprehensive agreement that both have scrupulously followed.

Strategies of threats sometimes lead to deadlock; the two sides demand terms that are mutually incompatible. The costs of deadlock can prompt one or both sides to rethink their preferences and shift to a more collaborative bargaining strategy. In October 1977, the Middle East peace talks had reached an impasse. The United States and the Soviet Union had been reduced to haggling over the wording of their communiqués and there was no prospect of any breakthrough. Frustrated and alarmed by the consequences of the deadlock, Anwar el-Sadat decided to change the structure of the negotiations by undertaking bilateral negotiations with Israel. By announcing his willingness to visit Israel, the Egyptian president hoped to put the peace talks on a more collaborative footing. He succeeded, and Sadat and Begin quickly worked out the framework of an agreement. They subsequently engaged in much hard bargaining over the residual details of an Egyptian-Israeli peace.

From Theory to Practice

The strategy of coordination rests on the premise that an outcome can be found that comes close to meeting the preferences of both or all sides in a negotiation. Sometimes you can infer whether this outcome is possible from the context of the negotiation. On other occasions it is not at all evident, and the first task of the bargainer is to ascertain the extent to which the parties have similar or reconcilable preferences.

To determine the applicability of the strategy of coordination, you need information about the preferences of the other parties. In a two-sided negotiation, you can attempt to gain this information by describing your objectives to the other side. You should convey your preferences without committing yourself to specific demands. Your description may elicit a similar description and provide the information you need to assess the probability of finding a satisfactory outcome.

If the other side is not forthcoming about its preferences, try asking what it wants from the negotiation. There is nothing unusual about such a request; in every bargaining encounter, information needs to be exchanged about preferences if any agreement is to be reached. This is usually done through offers and counteroffers. However, the strategy of coordination seeks to avoid offers and counteroffers at the outset, because they encourage the participants to treat one another as adversaries. It relies whenever possible on the direct exchange of information about preferences in the hope of finding areas of substantial agreement.

If preferences appear close enough to make the strategy of coordination feasible, there are two ways to proceed. The bargainers can enumerate all the issues on the table with the aim of identifying those on which agreement is possible without any, or with very little, bargaining. The more contentious issues—those in which preferences clash—can be put aside to be dealt with later.

By identifying issues on which agreement is easy, the bargainers emphasize their common interests, encourage expectations that coordination will advance those interests, and provide stronger incentives to find solutions to the contentious issues that remain. If it is possible to resolve some important issues at the outset, the incentive to reach an accommodation on the remaining issues will be that much greater. If no agreement is possible on important issues, the strategy of coordination is probably inappropriate.

An alternative approach also begins with a discussion of issues and preferences, but it then makes use of offers and counters to find possible accommodations. The dean and I did this in our negotiation. Our exploratory discussions provided the dean with the information about my preferences that he needed to put together offers that came progressively closer to maximizing our respective interests. This approach was attractive to the dean because he did not have to reveal so much about his preferences and constraints. Finding the best accommodation took a little longer, but this process protected other interests of the dean. The use of offers and counteroffers is best suited to situations where one party is constrained from putting all of its cards on the table or is uncomfortable, for whatever reason, with a less structured approach to bargaining.

When using offers and counteroffers, a bargainer following the strategy of coordination tries hard to avoid competitive bargaining. The parties should be encouraged to see themselves as participating in a cooperative game in which all sides are seeking the solution most advantageous to their interests. The purpose of the offers and counteroffers is not to get a good deal at the other side's expense but to elicit new information that will allow the side making the offers to fashion a more attractive offer. If the method is effective, the two sides will move progressively closer to the solution that maximizes their respective interests.

Either approach in the strategy of coordination will quickly expose areas of agreement and disagreement. Even the most carefully constructed offer is likely to leave the participants divided on issues where their preferences clash. The next step in the strategy of coordination is to address these areas of disagreement and, where possible, find acceptable accommodations.

On relatively unimportant issues, compromise is the obvious solution. Both sides can give way, or one side can give in on one issue in return for a concession on another. Compromises are best effected by making informal offers that embody the terms of the compromises. They might be accompanied by the suggestion, "Now that we have agreement on all the important issues, why don't we just split the difference on the less consequential issues that remain."

More important issues may also be amenable to compromise, but they often require more sophisticated solutions. Any or all of the following tactics can be used in pursuing such compromises:

Offer low-cost concessions. The cost of a concession to the party making it is not always the same as the perceived gain to the party receiving it. One way to foster accommodation is to find a concession that is highly valued by one side but relatively cost free for the other side to make. Commercial negotiations are frequently characterized by time constraints. It may be imperative for the buyer that a proposed contract to be executed by a given date. If the seller faces no comparable constraint, it may be able to accommodate the buyer at little or no cost. A colleague of mine recently hired a contractor who had submitted a slightly higher bid than his competitors but had guaranteed to complete the deck being built onto her back porch before her son's bar mitzvah. To accommodate her, the contractor rescheduled another, less urgent job. Chapter 7 explores this tactic in more detail.

Make trade-offs. It is sometimes possible to shake loose a concession by making a concession. This tactic links the resolution of the issue in question to that of one or more others. The party using this tactic tries to put together a package that both sides will consider attractive even though it would require both to make concessions. This tactic is also discussed in Chapter 7.

Reshape preferences. Hamlet opines that "there is nothing either good or bad but thinking makes it so." So it is with concessions. The cost of making them depends on the bargainer's understanding of the substantive and symbolic value of what is at stake. New information or interpretations of the bargaining encounter can prompt a reevaluation of the cost of making a concession or the value of receiving one. Astute bargainers can sometimes encourage the other side to undertake a reevaluation and to conclude that the desired concession is not nearly as costly as they had previously thought. As it is another application of the strategy of rewards, this tactic too is analyzed in Chapter 7.

Problems

The strategy of coordination only works when preferences are fundamentally similar or easily reconcilable. For the strategy to succeed, the parties must grasp this reality and work together to find an agreement that maximizes those interests. Not every bargainer is so perceptive or prepared to cooperate.

Because the strategy of coordination is unusual and to some bargainers a novelty, it will probably require some salesmanship to persuade parties to follow it. Initially reluctant or dubious bargainers can often be brought around by a good explanation of the strategy and the ways in which it is likely to benefit them. This explanation should emphasize the way in which the strategy seeks to maximize the common interests of the parties. It should also stress the exploratory nature of the strategy and how it is a low-cost or even no-cost option. If the parties find enough common preferences to proceed, fine. If not, they can think about ways of bridging the gap between them or begin to bargain more competitively.

People differ. Some are open and cooperative by nature and more likely to respond positively to the challenge of coordination. Other people are suspicious and secretive. This may be a reaction to previous bargaining encounters or relationships in which their openness was exploited. It will be more difficult to persuade such people that the strategy of coordination is in their interest.

GENERAL RULES

1. The strategy of coordination is least applicable to bargaining encounters dominated by the issue of price. In such encounters, one side's gain is generally equivalent to the other's loss, and it is impossible to harmonize preferences.
2. The strategy is most applicable to complex encounters in which many different issues are involved and most of them are not about price.
3. The greater the overlap in preferences on important issues, the easier it should be to find an accommodation.
4. The better the agreement on major issues, the more committed the

parties are likely to be to reach an accommodation on the remaining issues.

5. The strategy of coordination is easier to apply and more likely to work in situations where there is a degree of trust between the parties.

CHECKLIST

1. Explain the strategy of coordination and, if necessary, try to persuade the other side of its utility.

2. Determine the feasibility of the strategy by exchanging information about preferences.

3. Attempt to find a solution that harmonizes as much as possible the preferences of the parties.

4. If necessary, use offers and counteroffers to gain more information. Use this information to construct offers that better maximize the interests of the parties.

5. Try to bridge the remaining gaps by compromise, low-cost concessions, trade-offs, and reshaping of preferences.

Chapter 7

The Strategy of Rewards

The strategy of collaboration depends upon the exchange of information about preferences to find a mutually acceptable outcome. The strategy can work well when the preferences are not far apart. In many bargaining situations there is at best an imperfect fit between the preferences of the parties involved. To reach an accommodation, at least one side must be persuaded to accept an outcome that it would otherwise reject.

Persuasion can take two forms: threats to make rejection of a proposal too costly and rewards to make it more attractive. Both forms of persuasion assume that preferences reflect estimates of cost and gains and that they can be shifted in the desired direction by manipulating that calculus.

Threats of punishment and promises of rewards are not mutually exclusive strategies. Bargainers commonly rely on carrots *and* sticks to shape others' preferences. However, for the sake of clarity, we analyze the two strategies sequentially. This chapter looks at rewards; the next examines threats. Chapter 8 also describes how the two strategies can be combined, and the relationship of both to the strategy of coordination.

Enhancing the Outcome

The strategy of rewards attempts to make an outcome more acceptable by making it more attractive. There are a number of ways to do this.

Low-cost Concessions

Giving the other side what it wants is the most obvious way to make agreement more attractive, but it may also be the most costly. Someone shopping for a used car will want the dealer to drop his price. But any concession the dealer grants reduces his profit. Any gain by either side represents an equivalent loss to the other.

To finesse this problem, people sometimes open the bargaining with inflated demands. "Tailpipe Harry" hopes to realize $2,300 for a 1987 Toyota on his lot, but puts a $3,000 sticker price on it. He is prepared to come down as much as $700 to give the appearance of making a meaning-ful concession. By doing so, he hopes to convince a customer that the car is a "steal." With any luck, he may have to drop only $500 from the price to clinch the deal. A prospective buyer can play the same game and offer Harry $1,500, fully expecting to pay more to get the car.

Bargaining of this kind is characteristic of the bazaars of the Middle East. Everybody in the market knows the tactic of inflated bids and partici-pates in the ritual. In the bazaar, or anywhere else inflated bids are used, the point may be reached where neither seller nor buyer is willing to make any further concessions to close the remaining gap between them. One or both may threaten to walk away from the negotiations in the hope that it will promote the other side to make the concessions necessary to secure agreement. If neither side is bluffing, this tactic will fail.

Another way to bridge the gap is to expand the bargaining set by introducing a new issue. If the issue is important to the other side and you can satisfy it by making a concession at little or no cost, you may convince the other side to make a concession on the issue of interest to you. Tailpipe Harry might offer to throw in four used snow tires at no extra cost if the prospective buyer agrees to his price of $2,300. The tires have been lying around unsold for several years and will cost Harry nothing to give away. For the prospective buyer, a school teacher who lives at the top of a steep hill that can be extremely treacherous in winter, the tires represent a real bonus and may reconcile her to Harry's "rock bottom" price for the car.

A side payment can sometimes be advantageous to the party making it. In the Cuban missile crisis, President Kennedy wanted Soviet Premier Nikita S. Khrushchev to remove the missiles the Soviet Union had de-ployed secretly in Cuba. Khrushchev had justified the missiles as necessary to protect Cuba from American attack. Kennedy did not want to attack Cuba; he thought it would be a costly operation and risk war with the

Soviet Union. He readily acceded to Khrushchev's demand for a noninvasion pledge in return for withdrawal of the missiles. Kennedy was also pleased with the pledge, because it provided him with a compelling justification for exercising restraint in face of growing pressure from American hawks to invade Cuba.

In both examples, low-cost concessions in the form of side payments were made to reconcile initially disinclined people to a proposed accommodation. Tailpipe Harry's offer of the tires encouraged the school teacher to reappraise the utility of paying $2,300 for the Toyota. If snow tires were essential for winter driving, and new ones, even on sale, would cost at least $300, the real cost of the car would be only $2,000. In Cuba, Khrushchev insisted on a side payment to make withdrawal of the missiles more palatable. Because Khrushchev was absolutely convinced that the United States intended to attack Cuba, he regarded the noninvasion pledge as a significant gain.

Low-cost concessions sometimes take the form of an exchange of principle for substance. In many disputes, one of the parties may be willing to accede to the other's demands if its claims are recognized in principle. Former Kissinger aide Leslie Gelb was willing to drop his suit for damages when Kissinger agreed to apologize for wiretapping his telephone. Leonid Brezhnev was willing to accept certain limitations on the Soviet Union's strategic nuclear arsenal in return for American recognition of the USSR as a co-equal superpower. Israel returned the oil rich and strategically located Sinai Peninsula to Egypt in return for recognition and a peace treaty. In the first two cases, the symbolic concessions were relatively cost free to the side making them.

Linkage

Low-cost concessions generally require expansion of the bargaining set. One side introduces a new issue in the hope that agreement about it will facilitate agreement on the other issue(s) by making the overall package more attractive. Linkage tries to exploit the differential utility to the parties of concessions on the new issue. To the extent that the concession is low cost for the side making it but high value for the side receiving it, the latter is likely to upgrade its estimate of the utility of the proposed accommodation.

There are many different kinds of linkage. In our two examples, the parties expanded the scope of the bargaining by introducing new issues. Another possibility is to link the outcome to other bargaining encounters between the parties. This mechanism was used by the United States and Iran in 1980 to resolve the crisis between them. Washington wanted the release of the American hostages held by Iranian militants and the government. Teheran wanted its financial assets in the United States unfrozen. The deal, worked out with the help of Algerian intermediaries, satisfied both concerns: the hostages and assets would be released at the same time, although some Iranian funds would be held in escrow to settle expected American claims.

The USAir–British Airways negotiations of 1992 represent an unsuccessful effort at linkage. British Airways agreed to inject $750 million cash into the ailing USAir in return for 44 percent ownership but only 21 percent of the voting stock. The two airlines would combine their schedules in the expectation that USAir, with its extensive domestic routes, would feed millions of passengers bound for overseas destinations to British Airways. American, Delta, and United Airlines—the "Big Three"—lodged bitter protests with the Department of Transportation. They charged that British Airways would have an unfair advantage on the lucrative North Atlantic route by virtue of its code-sharing arrangement and de facto penetration of the American market.

Transportation Secretary Andrew H. Card, Jr., was initially untroubled by the merger but became increasingly critical in response to the public relations campaign waged by the Big Three and President Bush's concern not to alienate voters in a close presidential election. Card sought to assuage the Big Three and score points with voters by linking his approval of the merger to a grant by the British of more gates for U.S. carriers at London's Heathrow Airport. On 3 December, he announced that no deal was possible unless the British agreed forthwith to open their skies. The British government was unwilling to do this, and British Airways withdrew its offer to USAir. The two airlines were disappointed; they regarded their proposed merger as mutually advantageous (and would later negotiate a less ambitious arrangement that the Clinton administration would approve).

Bargainers can also invoke the "shadow of the future." If they bargain frequently, one side can encourage the other to make a concession in the current negotiation in return for a promise to reciprocate on a later occasion. One of my neighbors is an airline pilot who from time to time assumes heavier flying schedules in some months to give one of his colleagues more time off. They stand in for him when he wants extra free time. Arrangements like these require trust between the parties.

Delinking Issues

Sometimes, the cost associated with a concession is not intrinsic but lies in the negative implications the concession would have for relations with third parties. A company may resist giving a special price to a preferred customer for fear that it will provoke similar demands from other customers. A manufacturer may refuse a large wage increase demanded by a union out of concern that it will set an industrywide precedent. To get the concession, the party seeking it may need to find a way to limit its detrimental consequences for the other side. The preferred customer could promise never to reveal the price it paid and thus protect the seller from other demands for discounts. Union representatives might conspire with management to describe their wage increase as a unique response to unusual circumstances and not applicable to other wage contacts management must negotiate.

Salary negotiations frequently involve separation and secrecy. At an Ivy League university where I worked, faculty salaries were closely guarded secrets. Through a friend in the payroll office, I nevertheless discovered that other senior professors in my department were paid on average 15 percent more than I was. Having just received an offer of a chair from another university, I demanded a 20 percent salary increase. The university was retrenching because of financial constraints, but the dean of the arts college came across with 15 percent, on the grounds that I was a special case; he insisted that he was not granting a pay increase but a salary equalization. I was instructed to keep my mouth shut, so that other professors receiving disproportionately low salaries would not discover the situation and put in similar requests.

The Cuban missile crisis provides the most dramatic example of another possibility, a public-private deal. As noted earlier, President Kennedy agreed to issue a public pledge not to invade Cuba in return for the Soviets' withdrawal of their missiles from Cuba. Kennedy was also willing to dismantle the American Jupiter missiles he had deployed in Turkey, but he categorically rejected Khrushchev's demand for a public missile swap, because of its probable political consequences. Republicans, joined by dissidents from his administration, would accuse him of caving in to the

Soviets. On 27 October, at the height of the crisis, Robert Kennedy explained to Soviet ambassador Anatoliy Dobrynin that his brother was prepared to remove the missiles in Turkey within six months provided Moscow made no attempt to claim it as a concession. Khrushchev, who had been pushing for a public missile swap, insisted on a private letter from Kennedy acknowledging the understanding. Kennedy refused and Khrushchev did not push, because he had come to realize that secrecy was in his interest too. Cuban leader Fidel Castro was furious with him for agreeing to withdraw the missiles and would have been apoplectic if he had thought that Khrushchev had cut a deal beneficial to the Soviet Union at Cuba's expense.

To cover up the concession, the Kennedy inner circle invented the story that the president had asked to have the obsolete Jupiter missiles in Turkey removed before the crisis. Unbeknownst to the president, the State Department had dragged its heels, because the Turks were reluctant to give up the missiles. Kennedy was alleged to have exploded when he learned during the crisis that the missiles were still in place. Administration insiders told this tale to unsuspecting newsmen and later confirmed it in their memoirs.

If discovered, private deals can get the parties involved in big trouble, all the more so if they are illegal. In 1991, a big scandal erupted in Japan when it was revealed that leading Japanese investment firms had reimbursed major institutional clients for their losses in a falling stock market. Less favored clients received no such relief. The investment houses lost customers and had to pay heavy fines.

Context

Assessments of the costs and benefits of proposals are highly subjective and depend on the frame of reference brought to bear. If a couple who have put their house up for sale believe that the real estate market is going to improve markedly as the country comes out of a recession, they are likely to dismiss low offers out of hand. If they are convinced that housing prices are likely to stay stable or drop, an offer well below their asking price might be treated seriously and elicit a counteroffer.

By providing new information, different understandings of the context, or alternate frames of reference, bargainers can sometimes convince other parties to upgrade the value of a proposal they have previously spurned. Our school teacher will downgrade the value of the used car she is contemplating buying and lower the price she is willing to pay for it if she learns from the newspaper that the model in question is about to be recalled. Conversely, a multinational corporation attempting to purchase a small high-tech company that makes laser optical systems might be willing to make a higher bid if it learns that the company has just been awarded a multimillion-dollar contract.

The information in the previous examples was serendipitously discovered. Bargainers usually need actively to search for helpful information and communicate it to the other side. A lawyer I know recently arranged a buyout of another business for one of his firm's biggest clients. The proposed deal had complicated tax implications. He arranged for a nationally prominent tax lawyer to look into the problem, and that person identified all kinds of tax benefits that would accrue to both parties. His analysis clinched the deal. This morning, while picking up my car at the garage, I observed another variant of this tactic. An irate customer was complaining that he had been overcharged for the installation of a new timing mechanism. The service manager mollified him by showing him the bills of other customers who had paid the same price.

New information can also be used to get another party to back away from its demands. Several years ago, a colleague was audited by the IRS, who challenged her deductions for business travel. On the day of her interview, she arrived with a fully itemized and annotated list of travel expenses and receipts to back them up. The IRS agent shifted ground and questioned the relevance of the travel to her business of lecturing and writing. She substantiated the connection. The IRS agent offered her half the deductions. Feigning outrage, she insisted on all of them, and the agent reluctantly agreed.

Motives

Assessments of costs and gain are also influenced by others' readings of your motives. The question of motive will be paramount when the other side fears that any concession it makes will be exploited rather than reciprocated. A related fear is that a concession will convey an image of weakness and provoke further demands.

Both concerns drove Kennedy and Khrushchev at the outset of the Cuban missile crisis. Kennedy and his advisors regarded the secret Soviet missile deployment as a gratuitously aggressive provocation. They expected that if they backed away from their commitment to keep offensive weapons out of Cuba Khrushchev would become more brazen and challenge the Western position in Berlin. Khrushchev and his advisors subscribed to a mirror image of this expectation. They worried that if they withdrew the missiles in response to the blockade Kennedy would become more aggressive about exploiting his country's military advantage.

As the crisis progressed, Kennedy and Khrushchev learned more about each other's motives through their exchange of letters, secret meetings between Robert Kennedy and Ambassador Anatoliy Dobrynin, and the two countries' behavior on the blockade line. By clarifying their respective interests and reassuring the other about their intentions, Kennedy and Khrushchev changed each other's estimates of the cost of concession to the point where the costs were no longer seen as unacceptably high and the concessions appeared to hold out the prospect of substantial rewards.

From Khrushchev's perspective, the most significant form of reassurance that Kennedy practiced was self-restraint. Khrushchev was surprised that Kennedy did not exploit the missile crisis to overthrow Castro and humiliate the Soviet Union. Kennedy's forbearance reduced Khrushchev's fear that the president would use his country's nuclear superiority to try to extract political concessions. "Kennedy was a clever and flexible man," Khrushchev remarked afterwards. "America's enormous power could have gone to his head, particularly if you take into account how close Cuba is to the United States and the advantage the United States had in the number of nuclear weapons by comparison to the Soviet Union." *

The president's unexpected ability to restrain the American military encouraged Khrushchev to hope that American militants would not succeed in sabotaging détente with Kennedy as they had with Eisenhower. Kennedy's behavior altered Khrushchev's estimate of the possibilities for improved Soviet-American relations. From Khrushchev's new perspective, the expected costs of withdrawing Soviet missiles were greatly reduced and the possible rewards enhanced.

The crisis also redefined the context of Soviet-American relations for Kennedy. Khrushchev's restraint along the blockade line, his revealing messages, and Robert Kennedy's meetings with Dobrynin convinced him that the Soviet leader had bungled his way into a crisis he had not wanted and was desperately searching for a face-saving way to retreat. By Saturday night, when Kennedy approved a missile exchange, he was less fearful

---

*Interview with Alexei Adzhubei, Moscow, 15 May 1989; Nikita S. Khrushchev, *Khrushchev Remembers: The Glasnost Tapes*, trans. and ed. Jerrold Schecter (Boston: Little, Brown, 1990), p. 179.

that Khrushchev would interpret American concessions as a sign of weakness and respond by becoming more aggressive. He thought that there was some chance that the Soviet leader would see concessions as evidence of his commitment to avoiding war and to reciprocating with tension-reducing measures of his own. Kennedy and Khrushchev came to the conclusion that concessions might be more effective in achieving their goals than continued confrontation.

As in the missile crisis, concern about the reputational consequences of concessions is most likely to be found in repetitive bargaining encounters, where each side's estimates of the other's motives and resolve will influence its behavior in subsequent rounds. It can also become an issue in complex, one-time negotiations in which issues are dealt with sequentially—in effect, in repetitive bargaining encounters. The Uruguay round of GATT lasted six years; some of the participants reasoned that how they responded to issues that arose in the process would create expectations about their responses to subsequent issues.

Judgments about motives influence one-time encounters in different ways. When you buy a used car from someone you have never met before and are never likely to see again, you will probably have two concerns: the price and condition of the car. You should greet with suspicion all assertions by the owner that the car has been trouble free and a pleasure to drive. If it is such a great car, why is it up for sale? If the owner explains that she is going overseas for two years and it makes no sense to take her cherished car, and you see the "for sale" sign in front of her house, you may be more willing to credit her claims. All the more so, if she shows you a folder in which she has kept all the receipts for repairs, and urges you to speak with the local dealer, who services the car. Even so, it is wise to have it checked out by a qualified mechanic.

Our hypothetical car seller is practicing a variant of the strategy of rewards. By reassuring you about her motives for selling the car, she is trying to allay your concern that she is unloading a lemon. If she convinces you that the car has been trouble free and well maintained, you may be willing to pay a little more and meet her asking price. The money you can expect to save in repairs may more than compensate for the few hundred dollars extra the car costs up front. Both of you emerge as winners.

There are several ways to reassure others about your motives:

1. Whenever possible, requests for concessions should be accompanied by expressions of willingness to make some kind of reciprocal concession. This encourages the other side to credit your sincerity and fairness.

2. Always explain the reasons why you seek concessions or refuse to make them. Justify your position in terms of your needs and interests. Try to convince the other side that you are not asking for any gratuitous rewards, only for what you need or can reasonably expect to obtain. Be clear about the terms for which you are willing to settle. Reassurance of this kind encourages a more positive view of your motives and the expectation that meeting your demands will lead to agreement, not new demands.

3. When doubts about your sincerity are a major stumbling block to agreement, or perhaps even to negotiations, it may be necessary to make major concessions up front. Anwar el-Sadat did this in 1975, when he broke ranks with other Arab leaders and publicly expressed willingness to visit Israel and address its parliament. Sadat's announcement made him an instant pariah throughout the Arab world and cost Egypt billions of dollars in canceled foreign aid from oil-rich Saudi Arabia. Sadat's sacrifice convinced many Israelis of the sincerity of his interest in peace. He subsequently recouped his initial "down payment" through negotiations that led to Israel's return of the Sinai to Egypt.

4. Develop a reputation for honesty and for living up to your commitments. Concessions are meaningless unless they can be implemented. A reputation for honesty puts teeth into promises of rewards and makes them more valuable to recipients. People are often willing to pay more for better quality or service. My colleague buys her computers from a man who will come at a moment's notice to service them. She insists that it is worth every extra penny. Honesty and dependability are not only ethical, they offer real long-term rewards.

All of the tactics we have discussed are intended to make an outcome more acceptable to another party by making it more attractive. No one tactic is inherently superior; their relevance and utility are determined by the context of the bargaining. Experienced bargainers are quick to recognize the nature of other parties' concerns and to come up with relatively cost-free ways of addressing them. They may employ several of the tactics if it is necessary to secure an agreement.

When to Use the Strategy

The strategy of rewards can be used in a wide range of bargaining situations, either by itself or in tandem with other strategies. These possibilities include:

1. *With the strategy of coordination:* The strategy of coordination attempts to find a solution that matches as closely as possible the preferences of the parties. When the strategy works, it often leaves a residue of outstanding issues that must be resolved by compromise or some other means. One of these means is the strategy of rewards, relatively easy to apply in this situation because the prior success of the strategy of coordination will have created strong incentives to settle any remaining issues that stand in the way of accommodation.

   The strategy of coordination will have identified the issues that are problematic and provided both sides with adequate information about the other's preferences and needs. It is also likely to have fostered a spirit of mutual cooperation between the parties that will make them more receptive to and will facilitate the strategy of rewards.

2. *When the strategy of coordination has failed:* When preferences diverge markedly, attempts at coordination, no matter how skillfully managed, are unlikely to succeed. It then becomes necessary to fall back on other strategies. The strategy of rewards is an obvious choice, because it builds on the knowledge about preferences that the attempted strategy of coordination will have generated. The strategy of rewards should be applied to the important issues that coordination was unable to resolve. If it succeeds, you can move on to less important issues, possibly resolving those by compromise.

3. *In lieu of other strategies:* Negotiations often begin with both sides making their preferences known. This can be done informally, through a discussion of the issues during which each side tells the other something about the issues it wants to resolve and the kind of accommodation it envisages. Preferences can also be announced more formally, through the exchange of offers and counteroffers. Either way, the two sides will sooner or later discover where and by how much their preferences diverge.

   The key to applying the strategy of rewards is detailed knowledge about the issues that divide the parties. If you have previously pursued the strategy of coordination, much of that knowledge will already be at hand; the two sides will have exchanged information about their preferences and needs and will have identified the issues that are difficult to resolve and perhaps the reasons why this is so. Such information is harder to come by without a prior attempt at coordination. It is important not to use the strategy of rewards prematurely. Wait until discussion and an exchange of offers have identified the issues, preferences, and problem areas. Try to work through the issues and determine what, if any, agreements are attainable.

The appropriate moment to use the strategy is after an impasse has been reached and both sides begin to worry that agreement will be impossible to achieve. Waiting until this point in the negotiation offers two advantages: more information is available about issues, preferences, and needs, and the other side may be concerned enough about the possibility of nonsettlement to respond more positively to the strategy of rewards. Be careful not to wait too long. An impasse can harden into a confrontation and lead to threats and the exchange of harsh words, all of which make the strategy of rewards more difficult to apply.

4. *In tandem with the strategy of punishment:* Choosing between the strategies of punishment and reward is not an either-or choice. The two strategies are often employed together as part of a carrot-and-stick approach to bargaining. This is a time-honored technique of interrogators. Working as a team, one poses as the "bad cop" and uses force, or the threat of force, to try to coerce a confession from a prisoner. The "good cop" then enters the cell oozing kind words, reassurance, and, in the old days, cigarettes. He holds out the prospect of better treatment, even release, if the prisoner cooperates. Former KGB officers—who ought to know—insist that the alternation of terror and kindness is very effective in breaking down resistance.

Threats of punishment and promises of rewards are just as frequently coupled in business negotiations and international relations. In hostile takeovers, corporate raiders try to purchase enough stock to gain control of another company. They may offer directors of that company "golden parachutes," high paid positions in the new conglomerate, to persuade them to approve a low buyout bid. In the same breath, they may threaten to fire them forthwith if they reject the offer and the takeover bid succeeds. This approach is based on the recognition that the interests of the directors and the company are not necessarily the same and that greedy directors may be willing to sacrifice the company's interests for lucre.

Punishment and rewards can be used most effectively against a dependent target. In the 1973 Middle East War, Secretary of State Kissinger was able to wean Egypt away from the Soviet Union. Sadat was desperately trying to save the Egyptian Third Army, trapped on the far side of the Suez Canal and cut off from food and water by Israeli forces.

Kissinger indicated that he would leave the Third Army to its fate unless Sadat withdrew his request to Moscow for forces to help enforce the cease fire. If Sadat conceded in this, Kissinger would pressure Israel to withdraw its forces from both banks of the Suez Canal. Sadat quickly realized that Egypt would suffer greatly if he did not do as Kissinger wanted and could profit enormously by reorienting its foreign policy.

The successful use of threats and rewards requires impressive bargaining and interpersonal skills. You need to make accurate judgments about which issues are best resolved by rewards and which by threats. You must also manage the conflicting emotions that threats and promises can arouse. The other side, if angered by your threats, will be likely to react suspiciously to any offer of rewards you make and spurn any attempt to solicit information helpful in putting together such an offer. If rewards have resolved important issues, threats can seem very much out of place and provoke a stronger reaction than they would have otherwise.

It is easier to harmonize threats and rewards if threats are limited to nonsettlement, that is, the threat to walk away from the table if your conditions are not met. Such threats are usually much less provocative than threats of punishment. Chapter 8 examines both kinds of threats and describes how threats of nonsettlement can often be framed in a nonprovocative yet credible manner. Combining threats and rewards is still a tricky proposition. It is most likely to succeed against sophisticated bargainers who understand what you are trying to do and are able to keep their emotions from interfering with their judgment. It is best reserved for institutionalized bargaining, when you are dealing with professionals. Henry Kissinger's use of the strategy in 1973 is a good example.

Combinations of threats and rewards can also be appropriately used against a weak coalition. One or more members of the coalition can be offered rewards to encourage them to defect, making it easier to coerce the remaining member(s) with threats. Prosecutors routinely use this tactic when they offer members of a gang or conspiracy a reduced sentence in return for providing evidence or testimony against other members.

5. *When punishment has failed:* This is probably the most difficult situation in which to apply the strategy of rewards. Threats, especially those that are carried out, can transform a bargaining encounter into an

adversarial relationship. Revenge may become the other side's principal goal. In this circumstance, the promise of rewards is likely to be regarded as insincere or even as some kind of trap. Superpower relations during the Cold War offer repeated examples of this phenomenon.

Rewards can also be the most effective way of breaking a deadlock made worse by repeated use of the strategy of punishment. Mikhail Gorbachev's foreign policy is a case in point. By rewarding the West with a series of unilateral concessions (e.g., withdrawal from Afghanistan, unrestricted Jewish emigration, acceptance of NATO's "double zero" arms control proposal), the Soviet leader convinced Western publics and many Western leaders of his commitment to peace. He set in motion a reciprocal process that quickly and unexpectedly brought the Cold War to an end. More recently, Israel and the PLO have been trying to escape from their longstanding deadlock through a graduated strategy of rewards.

The Cold War and Arab-Israeli conflicts were both characterized by decades of hostility and deadlock. Repeated attempts to break the deadlock by punishment failed. These costly failures ultimately convinced thoughtful leaders that they would have to find some other way to resolve their differences. Suffering and learning finally combined to create conditions favorable to the implementation of the strategy of rewards. Alas, reaching this point took a long time, and in the Middle East there are many people on both sides who remain committed to confrontation.

From Theory to Practice

The first step in applying the strategy of rewards is to map the issues. Make a list of all the issues on the table and identify those most resistant to settlement. Ask yourself why these issues are difficult to resolve. Is it because the preferences of the two sides are so far apart? Is one side making demands that would prevent the other from meeting its minimal needs? Are any of these issues more important for one side than the other? Has either side linked the resolution of any issue to that of others?

With such a map, it is possible to determine if and how the strategy of rewards can be used. Examine unresolved issues for asymmetries that can be linked. The ideal situation is one in which different sides value different issues. By offering concessions on issues that are not so important to you but very important to the other side, it may be possible to get concessions on issues that are important to you. Kennedy offered Khrushchev a pledge not to invade Cuba in return for Soviet withdrawal of their missiles from the island. For a low-cost concession, Kennedy received a high-value reciprocal concession.

When both sides are concerned with the same issues, the strategy of rewards is more difficult to implement. In this situation it may be necessary to find a new issue that is important to the other side but on which you can make a low-cost concession. This is what Tailpipe Harry did. A single issue—price—dominated his negotiations with the school teacher. He succeeded in reconciling her to his asking price for the car by introducing the question of snow tires and making a concession that the school teacher valued highly.

By broaching a new issue, Tailpipe Harry expanded the bargaining set horizontally. Another possibility is to expand it vertically. If you expect to have other negotiations with the same party, there may be all kinds of possibilities for linking concessions by one party in the current negotiation to concessions by the other in future negotiations. Alternatively, either side can promise to do something valuable for the other side vis-à-vis a third party. The famous Anglo-French Entente of 1904 was concluded on this basis. France gave up any claims it had to Egypt in return for British promises to help convince Germany to recognize French colonial claims in Morocco. Creativity is needed in the search for links that will enable both sides to gain from agreement.

Linking issues of different values to the parties is the most direct and common use of the strategy of rewards. But it is unlikely to work when the two sides are equally concerned with the same issues. To break the resulting impasse it may be necessary to go a step further and inquire why the other side places so much emphasis on a particular issue.

Sometimes, the decisive consideration turns out to be the indirect cost of concessions. President Kennedy worried that if Khrushchev got away with sending missiles to Cuba, the Soviet premier would challenge him next in Berlin, where more important American interests were at stake.

It is sometimes possible to work with the other side to reduce the indirect costs of concessions. We have examined two tactics for doing this: delinking and private deals. They attempt to minimize the precedent-setting nature of concessions. Private deals can also protect the party making the concessions from retribution from important constituencies (e.g., spouses, business associates, public opinion).

Both tactics require active collaboration. The sides need to exchange information about their respective needs and how they can be met. Following agreement, they need to cooperate to put the desired "spin" on it, and they may need to misrepresent the terms of the agreement or keep all or part of them secret.

Common interest can provide the incentive for this kind of cooperation but there also needs to be trust. Delinking and private deals work best between parties who have a good relationship, but this is not always an essential requirement as the Kennedy-Khrushchev arrangement shows. When pursuing either tactic it is still advisable to do everything possible to encourage trust. For instance, explain how much it is in your interest to honor any agreement.

Assessments of costs are subjective and depend very much on the bargainer's frame of reference. By providing new information, different understandings of context, or alternative frames of reference, bargainers can sometimes convince other parties to upgrade the value of proposals they have previously rejected. For such new information to have effect, it must come from credible sources. Ideally, these sources are people who have professional standing and no interest in the outcome of the bargaining. When there is valid information in support of your argument, you should, if possible, get such a source to present the information and sketch out its implications. Alternatively, the other side should be encouraged to seek out a trusted source to verify what you say. If there is any documentation available (e.g., an independent study of the housing market), you should make it available to the other side.

Getting the Necessary Information

The strategy of rewards puts a premium on information. To apply it, you need to know as much as possible about how the other side evaluates the issues on the table, their off-the-table implications, and the frame of reference used to make these assessments. Using this information, it may be possible to construct and present an offer that will convince the other side to make concessions on the issues that are important to you.

The better the information, the more easily the strategy of rewards can be implemented. This is why the strategy is most effective in conjunction with the strategy of coordination. When the other side has been reticent about explaining its interests and how they are likely to be affected by the bargaining, using the strategy of rewards is more difficult but still possible.

Which issues the other side tables or refuses to discuss, its offers and counteroffers, and its reactions to your offers and counteroffers all provide information that can be used to make inferences about its interests. These inferences may or may not prove to be accurate, but they provide a starting point for the strategy of rewards.

Suppose you suspect that the other side is reluctant to accept your price because it is temporarily strapped for cash. You could propose a payment schedule that allows the other party to conclude the deal on the basis of a down payment. If the other side expresses interest in such an arrangement, you have guessed properly about its constraints, and follow-on bargaining about the size of the down payment and the schedule of payments may lead to an agreement. If the other side shows no interest or spurns your suggestion, you are probably on the wrong track. Try something else. Perhaps the stumbling block is its belief that agreement would set a damaging precedent. You could address this concern by proposing a private deal or agreeing to treat the negotiations as a special case.

The initial inferences you make about the other side's interests are a first approximation. The offers you make based on them may or may not address the other side's concerns. If not, little is likely to be lost, and the other side's response may provide additional information that will help you formulate a more effective strategy. It may take several attempts before you zero in on what is important to the other side.

Hit or miss application of the strategy of rewards can be costly. The other side can exploit you by pocketing all your concessions without budging an inch from its position. One way to guard against this is to make use of feelers. Instead of announcing that you are prepared to accept a down payment of 40 percent with the remainder to be paid over the course of the next eighteen months, you can ask the other side if the deal would be more attractive if some kind of deferred payment could be worked out. If it responds affirmatively, you can then proceed to negotiate the terms of the deferred payment, explicitly linking this concession to the other side's acceptance of your price. If the other side is not out to exploit you, feelers can be very helpful. They are informal, more easily cobbled together than full-scale offers, and thus can serve as an efficient way of teasing out what issues are important to the other side and how they might be addressed. With this information in hand, effective offers can more easily be constructed.

Whenever possible, feelers and offers should be preceded, accompanied, and followed up by direct questions to the other side with the intention of engaging it in a dialogue about its interests and concerns. Parties initially reticent to talk about their interests and concerns may begin to open up when they become convinced that you are prepared to stretch yourself to accommodate their interests and needs. The information they provide may be critical to your ability to offer the kind of reward necessary to convince them to accept your terms on the issues important to you. Feelers or offers used in tandem with questions are generally better at soliciting critical information than either used alone.

Frames of reference are more subtle constructs than interests and correspondingly more difficult to reconstruct and change. The starting point is the same: careful analysis of the actions and statements of the other side. You can also try to solicit information directly by asking how the other party views the negotiations, why it has rejected your offer, what motivates its counteroffer, or what it would like to achieve in the negotiations. Questions like these may elicit enough information to give you some insight into the broader perspective of the other side.

People are usually reluctant to alter or change their frame of reference. Nobody wants to be told that they are thinking about the problem in the wrong way or in a manner inconsistent with their real interests. We all want to believe that we understand our own interests better than others do. But people may nevertheless be grudgingly attentive to a well-constructed and gently presented argument indicating that their interests would be better served by a different frame of reference.

People are prone to think about bargaining encounters only in terms of the issues on the table. In such a mind-set, they will try to get the best deal they can on all those issues. This approach may be inconsistent with more important off-the-table interests. If those off-the-table interests would dictate different bargaining preferences, and those preferences would make more likely a concession you desire, you have an interest in broadening the other side's bargaining perspective. You can encourage consideration of more enduring or important interests, or even point out how the current approach to the bargaining may be contradictory to those interests. If your logic is compelling, the other party may reframe the bargaining and change its preferences.

Narrow or seemingly inappropriate frames of reference can also reflect the human tendency to avoid trade-offs among important values. People like to believe that their actions, policy preferences, or bargaining strategies advance all of their interests, not some at the expense of others. They tend to be insensitive to information that indicates that a choice is necessary and likely to resist any implication that there are contradictions in their bargaining goals. Your introducing those possibilities may nevertheless cause the other side to rethink its strategy and make it more receptive to proposals that would minimize its need to make unpleasant trade-offs.

People rarely switch frames of reference on the spot in response to new information or arguments. They need to accustom themselves to looking at a problem in a new or different light, and they may need to overcome whatever investment they have in their previous frame of reference. You need to proceed slowly and allow the other side ample time to digest your arguments and to work through the problem themselves. This is not a technique that can successfully be applied in short bargaining encounters or those subjected to severe time pressures.

GENERAL RULES

1. The strategy of rewards attempts to bridge gaps between preferences by reconciling the other side to your preferred outcome. It tries to make that outcome more attractive to the other side by reducing its estimate of the cost of concession or by rewarding it in some other way.
2. The strategy works best when multiple issues are on the table, when different issues are important to different parties, when low-cost concessions are regarded as extremely valuable by the side receiving them, and when one or both sides are concerned with the "shadow of the future."
3. The strategy is least applicable to zero-sum negotiations, like those about price. To resolve such negotiations by the strategy of rewards it will be necessary to introduce other issues, ones in which the cost of concession is low for one side and the value of receiving the concession high for the other.
4. Estimates of cost and gain are highly subjective and determined by the frame of reference. Parties to negotiations can sometimes be persuaded to shift their frames of reference and alter their preferences.

CHECKLIST

1. Use the strategy of coordination to reach agreement on as many issues as possible. Use the strategy of rewards to deal with residual issues.
2. Map the remaining issues on the table to identify those resistant to

settlement and determine the reasons agreement is difficult, the relative importance of the issues to the two sides, and the possible links among these issues. Decide which issues or terms are important to you and which, if any, you would be willing to concede to achieve your important objectives. Do the same for the other side.

3. Make an offer that exploits asymmetries you have discovered, to permit both sides, as far as possible, to realize their preferences on important issues in return for concessions on issues that are less important to them. If there are insufficient asymmetries, look for new issues to put on the table through which one or both sides can reward the other at low cost to themselves.

4. If no agreement can be reached, focus your attention on the outstanding issues and the ways in which the "shadow of the future" influences preferences. Explore the use of delinking and private deals to reduce the cost of concession.

5. If agreement is still elusive, consider the feasibility of shifting the other side's frame of reference. Is that frame of reference appropriate to or consistent with its interests? Can you suggest an alternative frame of reference that is better suited to the other side's interests and will encourage it to regard the concession you seek as less costly or the rewards you offer as more valuable?

Chapter **8**

The Strategy of Punishment

This is my final offer, take it or leave it.

A strike is unavoidable unless the company comes up with a better health care package.

We will not refinance your country's debt until you balance the budget and curb inflation.

Threats like these communicate and dramatize the consequences of non-settlement. They are intended to make the target rethink its preferences and grant concessions it has been unwilling to make.

Successful threats need to be *sufficient*. They must hold out the prospect of enough loss to make concessions more attractive than standing firm. A credible threat to terminate bargaining is sometimes sufficient to do this. In the United States, where legal fees and court costs are exorbitant, one or both sides to a dispute may be loath to go to court because of the expense. They may prefer to make concessions to obtain an out-of-court settlement. In other bargaining encounters, threats of punishment may be necessary to alter another party's preferences. "You'll never see your son alive again, unless you come up with the ransom money," the kidnapper tells the distraught parents. Labor-management disputes are often characterized by less violent but equally punitive threats. Preparing to strike against an employer, a union may attempt to organize sympathy strikes at other production sites owned by the employer. Management in turn may threaten to hire new workers to replace those who go on strike.

Threats must also be *credible*. When my younger son threatens to leave home if he cannot watch his favorite television program, I laugh. When the Internal Revenue Service threatens to levy a stiff fine unless I pay overdue taxes, I write a check. The IRS threat is credible; it comes from an organization with the resources and legal authority to punish me for noncompliance. I also recognize that the IRS computer that writes me threatening letters will continue to hound me if I refuse to pay. As the IRS example indicates, credibility is a function of *capability* and *resolve*. The party making a threat must have the resources and apparent commitment to carry it out.

Capability is generally easier to demonstrate (and to assess) than resolve. Sometimes it speaks for itself. A governmental agency may have a large legal staff that makes it relatively inexpensive for them to take an unresolved dispute to court. In other situations, it is necessary to dispel any doubts about your ability to carry out your punitive threat. In labor-management disputes, a union may make it known that it has a large strike fund or that it has promises from other unions on whom the company depends to strike in support. Management may try to intimidate the union by preparing to shift manufacturing out of the country.

Demonstrations of capability can influence estimates of resolve. In war-threatening crises, leaders routinely mobilize their armed forces, to convey their commitment to use force. They also mobilize domestic and foreign support to show that their citizens and allies are behind them. Leaders can also try to make war unavoidable if the other side does not give in. They do this by courting loss of control.

In the Cuban missile crisis, President Kennedy went on television to promise the American people that he would not tolerate Soviet missile bases in Cuba. His real audience was the Kremlin. He was putting Soviet leaders on notice that he had burned his political bridges and staked his political career on getting their missiles out of Cuba. Kennedy also instituted a blockade of Cuba and mobilized overwhelming air, naval, and ground forces in preparation for a possible invasion. The blockade and American overflights of Cuba also imparted a degree of autonomous probability to the threat of war by raising the prospect of runaway escalation.

Similar methods are sometimes employed to demonstrate resolve in commercial disputes. Not long after the missile crisis, tenants in my New York City apartment house organized to compel a recalcitrant landlord to carry out necessary repairs. When it became apparent that negotiations were getting nowhere because the landlord doubted our capability and resolve to make him bring our building into compliance with the housing code, we swung into action on two fronts. One of the tenants, an attorney, filed a suit on behalf of the tenants' association to compel the city to take action against the landlord. Most of the tenants agreed to pay their rent into an escrow account. To attract media attention, we prepared to suspend tin cans on rubber tubes from the windows of our eighteen-story building, as a substitute for the nonfunctioning intercom. This ploy was unnecessary. Within two days of filing suit and beginning to withhold rent, the landlord signed an agreement with the tenants' association committing himself to the necessary repairs.

Credibility is more difficult to establish when the threat is costly to the party making it. Before divorce law in New York State was reformed, an ex-husband who was behind in his alimony payments could be sent to debtor's prison. Under the earlier law, a threat to withhold alimony was two-edged: the former wife would incur immediate financial loss, but the ex-husband would risk imprisonment unless he fled the state. Strikes are also uncertain weapons. If the strike is a long one and the union's treasury is rapidly depleted, the workers may suffer more than will management.

President Clinton's confrontation with China provides a textbook illustration of how difficult it can be to establish credit in a situation where the cost of threat implementation is high for both sides. As a candidate, Clinton had to woo important constituencies by promising the AFL-CIO and Senate Majority Leader George Mitchell that he would terminate China's most favored nation (MFN) trading status if it did not end its human rights abuses. Once elected, Clinton persuaded Senate Democrats to formally allow him to draft a more flexible executive order. Signed on 28 May 1993, it renewed China's MFN status for a year but imposed two "mandatory" conditions for any further extension: Peking had to allow emigration of close family members and comply with a 1992 agreement banning export to the United States of products made with prison labor. China was also urged to make progress on several other human rights issues.

Economists predicted that China's exports to the United States would decline by more than 50 percent if its MFN status was revoked. Clinton's threat was never taken seriously by the Chinese, who recognized that there was no consensus in the United States on a hard-line human rights policy. Over the next few months, Peking sold Iran chemicals for making weapons, exported proscribed missile technology to Pakistan, and rejected U.S.

pleas to cancel an underground nuclear test. As Sino-American relations deteriorated, the American business community, fearful of losing lucrative contracts, mobilized against Clinton's policy. The National Association of Manufacturers demanded that trade and human rights be uncoupled. Some influential figures within the administration, including former ambassador to China Winston Lord, urged the president to substitute a policy of incentives for one of threats.

When threats are costly, special efforts are required to impart credibility to them. Threat makers can try to hide the costs to themselves or attempt to convince the other parties that these costs are less than they think or that they are fully prepared to accept them. A friend of mine went through an acrimonious divorce in the 1960s and was taken to court for refusing to pay alimony to a woman who was quite capable of supporting herself. When the court ordered him to pay, he refused and was threatened with debtor's prison. The following morning, he appeared at the office of his ex-wife's attorney with a suitcase, typewriter, and research notes, all set to go to jail and use the time to finish a book he was working on. The parties very quickly reached a settlement. My friend later told me that his bravado collapsed as soon as he left the law office; he shook all the way home.

Perhaps the most effective means of establishing credibility is to convince the other side that whatever the cost of the threat it will be costlier still not to implement it. To do this, you need to show how concession would seriously damage more important interests. The same tactic can be used by the targets of threats to explain why they cannot give in. China rejected outright President Clinton's demand for changes in their human rights policy. They spread the word informally that any bending to U.S. pressure would embolden their internal opposition and bring new demands from dissident groups and nationalists. The Japanese government resisted Clinton's demands for trade concessions on similar grounds.

Threats that undeniably involve great cost can still be made credible. In nineteenth-century Japan, rural tenants were known to disembowel themselves in front of the gates of their landlord's home to shame him and dramatize their grievances. When enough tenants had bloodied enough doors, the threat to commit suicide became credible and effective. Superpower nuclear deterrence was based on the threat of national suicide. If the Warsaw Pact countries invaded Western Europe the United States was pledged to attack the Soviet Union with nuclear weapons. But by the later 1960s, this would have provoked Soviet nuclear retaliation against the

United States. In effect, American leaders threatened to destroy the United States to protect Western Europe. Many Europeans, Charles de Gaulle among them, publicly scoffed at the notion that the United States would sacrifice New York for Hamburg or Paris. For their part, American officials doubted that the Europeans would let them use their nuclear weapons, for fear that their countries would become the targets of Soviet nuclear retaliation.

Rational people may make irrational threats, but only irrational people are expected to carry them out. Richard Nixon consciously fostered an image of himself as irresponsible, in the hope of imparting credibility to American nuclear threats. Evidence that has become available since the end of the Cold War indicates that nuclear deterrence was far more robust than either superpower imagined. Leaders on both sides were terrified by the prospect of nuclear war and worried that their adversary was aggressive, risk prone, and irrational. Richard Nixon's efforts represented psychological overkill.

Superpower nuclear deterrence also rested on what one prominent analyst called "the threat that leaves something to chance." Neither superpower could credibly threaten nuclear war, but either could alert its strategic and conventional forces in response to threatening behavior by the other. Alerted forces, especially those in close proximity, would be at greater risk of causing an incident that could rapidly escalate into an all-out military confrontation. This almost happened during the Cuban missile episode, when Soviet forces in Cuba, acting against Moscow's orders, shot down an American U-2 reconnaissance aircraft. President Kennedy was under great pressure from his political and military advisors to launch retaliatory attacks against Soviet antiaircraft forces in Cuba. He nevertheless exercised restraint, out of concern that retaliation would provoke more incidents and compel him to launch further attacks against Cuba, possibly leading to a Soviet-American war.

President Kennedy was able to exploit the risk of war to his country's advantage. On Saturday night, the 27th of October, he sent Robert Kennedy to warn Soviet ambassador Anatoliy Dobrynin that he was under enormous pressure to attack Cuba and he needed within twenty-four hours a Soviet decision to withdraw the missiles. The president had no intention of ordering an air strike or an invasion, but his threat was credible and frightening to Moscow because an American attack would overwhelm Soviet forces in Cuba. If Moscow accepted defeat, the Soviet Union and the leader would be humiliated. But horizontal escalation in the form of an air attack against American missiles in Turkey would risk rapid escalation and raise the prospect of nuclear war. Soviet premier Khrushchev hastened to reach an accommodation.

Estimates of credibility are also influenced by past behavior. If the party making a threat has carried out its threats in the past when its demands have been rejected, its threats will be more likely to be seen as credible. Contrast, for example, the behavior of the Internal Revenue Service with that of the Immigration and Naturalization Service (INS). The former has a reasonably good record of discovering and prosecuting tax evasion and fraud. The latter is known to be hopelessly inefficient and inept. Fear of getting caught and punished deters many people from cheating on their taxes. Lack of respect for the INS encourages illegal immigration and the businesses that bring immigrants into the country illegally.

Probably the best example of the consequences of failing to carry out threats is NATO in Yugoslavia. In 1994, Bosnian Serb forces began a counteroffensive against Bihac and its surrounding territory despite NATO warnings of retaliatory air strikes. With United Nations' approval, NATO planes attacked a Bosnian Serb airfield, but they were careful not to destroy any of the planes on the tarmac. The Serbs continued their offensive. Not long afterwards, the United Nations' representative recalled a second air strike by NATO when its planes were already airborne and on their way to the target. The Western alliance's inaction convinced Bosnian Serbs that they not only could advance against Bihac with impunity but could interfere with UN relief convoys to the city and shoot at NATO forces without fear of retaliation.

Bargaining Asymmetries

In most bargaining encounters, both sides would be better off with an agreement. If not, one or both would have pursued their interests by other means. A threat to walk away from the table therefore raises the prospect of loss to both sides. Such threats are more credible when the side that makes them will suffer less from nonsettlement. Relative advantage of this kind is due to structural asymmetries in the bargaining situation.

Asymmetries are inequalities in the context of the bargaining or in the needs of the bargainers. Among the more important of these asymmetries are the following:

The need to settle. The possibility of nonsettlement is present in every bargaining encounter. Bargainers generally recognize that neither they nor their opposite numbers are willing to make agreements that would leave them worse off than having no agreement. In some circumstances, this has little effect on the negotiations. If I go to an antique store hoping to buy an old cherry dining room set but prepared to live quite comfortably without it if I have to pay more than $800, I am fully prepared to walk out of the shop if the owner insists on a substantially higher price. It was fun in any case to look at the furniture and get some idea of what is available at what price. And moreover, the store was comfortably air conditioned.

In other bargaining encounters, one or both sides are very keen, perhaps desperate, to reach an agreement. In this circumstance, the possibility of nonsettlement may hang over the negotiations like the sword of Damocles. The bargaining may be influenced at every step by concern to avoid a rupture. A childhood friend of mine fled Vienna with his parents one step ahead of the Nazis. To cross the frontier to the relative safety of Italy they had to bribe the Austrian border police. The police demanded some outrageous sum and my friend's father did his best to bargain them down, but there was no question, he later told his family, that he would have paid whatever was necessary get them across the border. The alternative was too horrible to contemplate.

Most bargaining encounters lie somewhere between these two extremes. Nonsettlement is an outcome one or both sides would like to avoid, and within reason, they are willing to discuss issues, frame demands, and offer concessions to secure an agreement. To the extent that either party sees its interests as best served by agreement, it becomes vulnerable to threats of nonsettlement by the other side.

Resources. More money in the bank, a larger strike fund, access to free or cheaper legal counsel, influential friends in the right places, more powerful military forces—such conditions can make nonsettlement less costly and threats of punishment easier to implement. In a divorce, if one party can more easily afford to take the case to court, a threat to do so is fully credible and offers that party the opportunity of obtaining a more favorable agreement. Most separated or divorced women find themselves on the short end; they are worse off than their former husbands and unable to afford the costs of litigation. They are often forced to settle for less than they would be awarded by a court.

Alternatives. The possibility of obtaining one's objectives by other means can confer a significant bargaining advantage, because it too reduces the cost of nonsettlement. The advantage will be more pronounced if the other side has no comparable alternatives. Companies in surplus labor markets regularly exploit this asymmetry to negotiate low wage rates with workers or their unions. The companies can make take-it-or-leave-it offers in the expectation that there is no shortage of other available workers. Workers who reject their offers may find it difficult, perhaps impossible, to find alternative employment.

Time. One side is often subject to time constraints, or more serious time constraints than the other side has. This vulnerability can frequently be exploited. In our negotiations with the Mazda dealer, we knew that time worked to our advantage in two ways. With 1995 models beginning to reach the showroom, the 1994 models dropped in value. At the end of each month, the dealer had to pay a fee to the manufacturer for all the cars on his lot. We waited until the '95 models had been on display for two months and the dealer was increasingly desperate to unload his remaining '94 cars. We also waited until the second to last business day of the month to do our bargaining. We arrived at the dealer with a bank draft for the amount we were willing to pay (including tax and tag transfer fee), making it possible to drive the car off the lot that afternoon. The Russians played a similar game with George Bush after he lost the 1992 presidential election. Bush was extremely keen to sign the START II arms control agreement before leaving the White House. The Russians dragged out the negotiations to extract last minute concessions from an increasingly frantic lame-duck president.

Precedent. Repetitive bargaining encounters on the same issues create expectations about the general shape of any agreement. Terms at variance with these expectations are more difficult to justify and may permit the other side to threaten more credibly to walk away from the table, especially if it is prepared to accept a settlement within the generally expected zone of agreement. If houses in a certain block are more or less similar and on lots of the same size, a prospective buyer can readily determine the market value of a house that has just come on the market by looking at the price for which other houses on the block have recently sold. Other things being equal, a couple who asks significantly more for their house can price themselves out of the market. Any well-informed buyer will reject their asking price, make a lower counteroffer, and, if that is rejected, make an offer on another house.

Precedent is also important in disputes where there are legal remedies. Courts uphold the law by applying legal precedent to the cases before them. The side that can make the better claim to be acting in accord with precedent is likely to fare better in court. In governmental, commercial, and personal disputes, lawyers routinely urge their clients to settle out of court when they think legal precedent favors the other side.

Reputation. Individuals, organizations, or governments with a reputation for toughness or irrationality may be able to make more convincing threats to break off negotiations. Some students of bargaining suggest that it is useful, even imperative, to establish a reputation for toughness, even if this requires passing up settlement in one or more bargaining encounters. The costs of nonagreement, the argument goes, can be more than recouped in subsequent encounters if a reputation for toughness lends credibility to threats and results in a more favorable settlement. This tactic is most likely to succeed when the bargainer has a near monopoly over the object of the negotiations. If the commodity is available from other parties, who do not have the same reputation for toughness, the bargainer who has developed a reputation for resolve only damages its chance of doing business.

A reputation for skill or success can also enhance the credibility of threats. The plaintiff whose attorney has recently won millions of dollars of damages for clients in previous personal injury cases may be offered a more favorable out-of-court settlement than someone in comparable circumstances but with unknown counsel. The same is true for a successful book agent who is almost certain to secure a greater advance from a publisher than an unknown author could. Agents justify their profession on this basis.

Interests. This asymmetry cuts both ways. The side with less at stake can more convincingly threaten to walk away from a negotiation. A colleague of mine went shopping for a rug in Istanbul last year. The tourist trade had been in a slump and rug sellers were anxious to make a deal. My colleague, not desperate to buy a rug, was prepared to go home without one if she failed to find something she absolutely adored. Her nonchalance encouraged repeated concessions by rug dealers hoping to clinch a sale. Unfortunately, she failed to find an irresistible kilim of the right size.

The side that has more at stake can also make credible threats not to settle for an outcome that would seriously compromise its interests. A government publicly committed to fighting inflation by restraining wage increases can more credibly reject union demands. However, this is a risky strategy because of the costs of failure. In 1991, the German government refused to consider any wage increase above the inflation rate and subsequently lost standing in the polls when federal workers went on strike in protest.

Willingness to suffer. In nineteenth-century San Francisco, disputes among patricians were settled by pistol duels. The death toll was horrendous, and the city fathers adopted a Native American substitute: disputants met outside the Presidio high above San Francisco Bay and competed with each other in throwing silver dollars out into the bay below. The contest continued until one of the disputants ran out of money, or—more often—refused to squander any more of his wealth. The side with more resources had an obvious advantage, but sometimes the winner was the side who felt more aggrieved and was more willing to part with his resources to achieve satisfaction.

Willingness to do without and suffer, if necessary, for the sake of one's honor, principles, reputation, or interest is an asymmetry in its own right that can be exploited in bargaining. I have already described how my friend obtained concession by giving the appearance of being ready to go to jail in defense of his principles. The same tactic has been widely used by American civil rights movements. By facing down hostile mobs and baton swinging police and filling the jails, proponents of racial integration rendered useless the most powerful weapons segregationists could muster. Local and state authorities had no choice but to address African-American demands for justice.

In the winter of 1994–95, Chechens engaged in a fight to the death against Russian invaders of their homeland and capital city of Grozny. Their willingness to suffer was their principal weapon against the more numerous and better-armed Russians. Chechens are hoping to inflict enough casualties on Russian forces to compel President Yeltsin to agree to their independence. The United States faced a similar situation in Vietnam, where American forces won every battle but lost the war. The Vietnamese who fought against them were willing to die in large numbers; the American people were not. Public dissatisfaction with the war forced President Johnson from office and ultimately compelled his successor to withdraw American forces from Indochina.

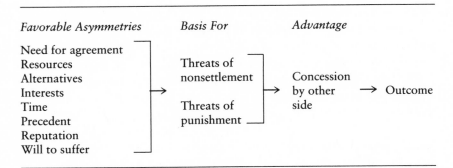

Figure 3. The Strategy of Punishment

Asymmetries are sometimes reinforcing. Resources, alternatives, and time, for example, may favor the same side, giving it a significant bargaining advantage. Prospective buyers of new American cars were in this situation in the late 1980s. Dealers were stuck with more cars than they could sell and were willing to cut prices to remain competitive. Customers were often able to shop around and negotiate a good deal.

When asymmetries are crosscutting, one or both sides may base threats of nonsettlement on different relative advantages. One side may try to exploit the other's known need for a quick settlement. That side may publicize its alternatives and corresponding unwillingness to settle for anything less than it is asking. It may be very difficult to determine who, if anyone, has the advantage. This is what happened in the 1992–93 Pittsburgh newspaper strike. The unions thought they had an advantage because of public support for the delivery boys, whose services the newspapers wanted to dispense with, and the weak finances of one of the two newspapers. The newspapers reasoned that the public would support their efforts to trim costs by reducing surplus labor and would turn against the unions if they went on strike. Neither side was willing to give in to the other's threats. In the long strike that ensued, public opinion was divided, one of the newspapers folded and, as a result, many more workers lost their jobs.

Punishment or Nonsettlement?

The strategy of punishment tries to compel the other side to accept your terms by making their rejection too costly. Toward this end, it employs threats of nonsettlement, punishment, or both.

It is important to bear in mind the distinction between threats of nonsettlement and threats of punishment. Threats of nonsettlement are much more common, easier to make, and generally more successful than threats of punishment. The possibility of nonsettlement is part and parcel of every bargaining encounter. All but the most ignorant bargainers recognize that neither they nor their opposites will make agreements that leave them worse off than having no agreement. Threats of nonsettlement are generally regarded as a legitimate way of communicating one's bottom line. Threats of punishment, by contrast, may arouse anger. They promise harm beyond the costs of nonsettlement and are likely to be seen as an egregious form of blackmail.

Threats of punishment are also more unpredictable. They can transform a bargaining encounter into a confrontation in which demonstrating firmness or getting revenge becomes more important than achieving agreement. Threats of punishment should be contemplated only when the strategies of coordination and rewards are inappropriate or have failed. Even then, there is a limited range of situations in which the strategy of punishment is likely to succeed.

There are some exceptions to the above generalizations. In marriages and families, where consensus is highly valued, a categorical refusal to reach agreement if your demands are not met will be regarded as selfish and disruptive. Conversely, there are some bargaining situations in which threats of punishment are an acceptable currency. In commercial negotiations, people routinely threaten to take their business elsewhere unless they get better service or a better price. In industries characterized by hard bargaining, management and labor would be surprised if the other did not threaten a strike or a lockout.

Threats of Punishment

Threats of punishment can be used to augment threats of nonsettlement and are most commonly made after threats of nonsettlement have failed. They attempt to compel concessions by holding out the prospect of greater loss to the other side.

Asymmetries are exploited in threats of punishment. A threat to go to court may capitalize on the greater financial resources of the party making the threat or on its belief that legal precedent favors its claim. Threats of harm to a company's business may be based on control of critical raw materials or on influence with major customers. Threatening to go to war may take advantage of a country's superior armed forces and industrial base.

Threats of punishment are more likely to arouse anger than threats of nonsettlement, and their impact cannot be so easily softened by the manner of their presentation. Threats that arouse anger risk failure. The target can become less rather than more pliable, and more committed to demonstrating that it cannot be coerced than to finding an acceptable accommodation. Henry Kissinger's emotional response to Leonid Brezhnev's threat during the 1973 Middle East War is a case in point. Brezhnev's goal was to compel the United States to restrain Israel. Before the Brezhnev message, Kissinger had been trying to do this; he had summoned Israeli ambassador Simcha Dinitz to his office several times to insist that Israel honor the cease-fire. Once he received Brezhnev's message, Kissinger's primary goal became avoiding any appearance of weakness. He halted his efforts to restrain Israel and convinced his colleagues to order a strategic nuclear alert. This shift in policy provoked the Soviet-American crisis that Brezhnev had been so eager to avoid.

Threats of punishment are most appropriate in situations (1) where you have a lot at stake, (2) where the other side has much less at stake, (3) the relationship is unimportant, and (4) the other side has an obvious vulnerability that can be exploited. Punishment is an uncertain instrument, but these are the conditions in which it is most likely to succeed. In the absence of any condition, success will be correspondingly more difficult.

The magnitude of your threat should be determined by the magnitude of the concessions you seek. You need to hold out the prospect of enough loss for the other side to conclude that it would be better off accepting your terms. The more important the interests the other side has at stake, the harder this will be.

The other side's interests are often opaque, and your threats can affect them in ways you cannot predict. For this reason, it is advisable, when possible, to use graduated threats. Start with a threat that seems appropriate and be prepared to escalate. Be careful to avoid overkill at the outset, because it is likely to antagonize the other side and may stiffen its resistance.

There is one exception to this rule. Bargainers are sometimes unwilling to make concessions because they cannot afford to appear weak in the eyes of important third parties. They may also resist because they know they cannot sell the concessions to these parties. Overwhelming threats of loss can sometimes help them to justify concessions and win support for them. Needless to say, overkill should be used only when there are clear indications that the other side is prepared to make concessions if it can deal with its constituency problem. In this circumstance, grave threats represent a form of tacit cooperation.

It should be pointed out that not all threats of punishment are intended to compel concessions. Some, like the Austrian ultimatum to Serbia in 1914, are meant to fail. Serbia's rejection of Austria's conditions would justify war, and Austrian prime minister Berchtold spent a sleepless night worrying that the Serbs might nevertheless find a way to accept his Draconic ultimatum. In business disputes, threats of punishment are also used to provoke a break and force a dispute into court or before some other body with the power to resolve it.

Do I Want to Make a Threat?

Before making a threat, you need to consider if it is in your interest to do so. If the answer is yes, you need to decide what kind of threat is appropriate and the best way to communicate it to the other side. You should also consider the consequences of success and failure.

The first and most important question is whether it is in your interest to make a threat. Sometimes this is easy to determine. The price you are offered is too high or more than you want to pay, and you will lose nothing by making a take-it-or-leave-it counterproposal. Other situations are more ambiguous, because of the many imponderables associated with threats. The biggest uncertainty surrounding a threat is usually its outcome; the other side can give in, make counterthreats, or walk away from the negotiations. To determine the advisability of a threat, you therefore need to consider the relative costs and gains of success and failure, and the likelihood of either outcome.

What If My Threat Succeeds?

Most threats are intended to succeed, and the people who made them are pleased when they compel important concessions or agreement. These immediate gains can have longer-term payoffs. A successful threat may set an important precedent for future negotiations or establish or maintain your reputation for toughness in the eyes of important constituencies. Tote up all your expected gains on the plus side of the ledger.

Successful threats can have costs. Your threat can arouse anger if the target regards it as inappropriate or is compelled to give up something of value. The other party may reconsider its relationship with you. If that relationship has been rewarding, the short-term gain conferred by a successful threat may bring more substantial long-term loss. You need to think about the nature of your relationship with the target. Is the party likely to be angered by your threat? If so, will its anger damage your relationship? Is the relationship worth preserving?

Successful threats can also antagonize third parties if they believe that you are bullying a weaker adversary. In business and international relations, this can lead to balancing or bandwagoning. Balancing is when third parties form a coalition against you. Bandwagoning is when they try to placate you or buy you off. Which outcome, if either, is your threat likely to have?

What If My Threat Fails?

If your threat fails, you are still likely to bear all the costs you would have if it had succeeded. You must add to these the costs of failure. If your threat fails, you have three choices: you can terminate negotiations, make a more serious threat, or accept the other side's best offer. When other alternatives are readily available, the choice may be obvious. You can move to the next fruit stall or used car lot and begin bargaining again. When there are no other attractive alternatives, the collapse of negotiations can entail substantial costs. You may have been substantially better off with the terms the other side was prepared to accept than with no agreement at all, but if you turn around and accept terms you had previously spurned, you expose your threat as a bluff.

In one-time negotiations, if your reputation is not on the line, it is not so damaging to have a bluff exposed. If your threat fails to compel a concession, you may be able to back away from it and conclude an agreement on the basis of the other side's last offer. In negotiations that are widely publicized or with people with whom you deal repeatedly, your bargaining reputation is important. Called bluffs will make it that much more difficult for you to make credible threats in the future.

On occasion, unsuccessful threats can have positive payoffs. They can demonstrate toughness to important constituencies or third parties with whom you must subsequently negotiate. If those negotiations are more important than the current one, sending a powerful message about your resolve not to sacrifice important interests may be worth the price of a failed threat and nonagreement. In toting up your expected costs of failure, you may need to consider both sides of the ledger.

Will My Threat Succeed?

Successful threats are sufficient and credible. They leave no doubt that rejection of your terms will prove more costly than their acceptance.

How potent a threat it takes to make rejection unappealing will depend on the nature of the concession sought. If the other side is only marginally disposed to rejecting your terms, small increments of additional cost conveyed by a threat may make acceptance preferable to rejection. If the target regards your terms as seriously adverse to its interests, the increment of cost imparted by the threat must be correspondingly greater. To calculate the level of threat required, you need to develop some conception of how the other side evaluates its interests and the consequences of accepting or rejecting your terms.

Generally speaking, threats are most effective against parties who are being asked to sacrifice only minor interests. Moderate threats, if they are credible, may succeed in this circumstance. When more important interests are at stake, more potent threats are required. When vital interests are on the line, threats, no matter how severe, are likely to fail and prove counterproductive.

Take the example of a clothing manufacturer who has rejected a low bid by a wholesaler. If selling at that price would represent a loss, threats of nonsettlement by the wholesaler will fall on deaf ears, unless, of course, the manufacturer is trying to unload excess stock and is prepared to take a loss. Threats of punishment—"I will take my business elsewhere in the future"—are also likely to fail, because to concede would set a dangerous precedent. The wholesaler, and perhaps other buyers as well, would be encouraged to demand low prices in all future negotiations.

The failure of credible threats is even more dramatic in politics, where individuals, groups of people, or nationalities have frequently been willing to sacrifice their lives for the sake of their religion, ideology, or way of life. Threats against core values are more likely to galvanize opposition and intensify resolve than they are to cow the people against whom they are directed.

Credibility's prerequisite elements, capability and resolve, both ultimately exploit asymmetries in your favor. The more favorable those asymmetries, the less it costs you to carry out the threat, the more it costs the other side if you do. For both reasons, your threats are likely to be taken more seriously. To design a credible threat, you should start by making a list of all the asymmetries relevant to the bargaining. The more these asymmetries favor you, the easier it will be to make a credible threat.

The nature of the asymmetries should also dictate the character of the threat. Threats of nonsettlement are most effective when the other side needs an agreement and has few, if any, alternatives for advancing or protecting its interests. If nonsettlement will bring it additional costs (e.g., bad publicity, loss of business, expensive law suits) your threats will be more potent still. Indirect threats of nonsettlement in the form of stalling or dragging out negotiations put pressure on parties that face deadlines.

If the other side has few interests at stake or has other ways of satisfying those interests, threats of nonsettlement will not be effective. Threats of punishment may be necessary to compel concessions. The most effective threats exploit some vulnerability of the other side, and it is worth making the effort to get as much information about the other side's situation as possible in the hope of discovering an appropriate pressure point. Needless to say, the other side can be expected to do its best to hide any vulnerability.

Making a Decision

In working through your decision, you need to consider the relative costs and gains of success and failure and the probability of both outcomes. This analysis may point to an obvious conclusion. If a successful threat would bring only marginal gains, but an unsuccessful one big losses, it is not in your interest. If a successful threat would bring substantial gain (or help you avoid substantial loss), while failure would leave you no worse off, a threat may be in your interest.

Such an accounting is not always clear cut. The costs and gains may be more evenly balanced, or they may turn on the outcome of the threat, and that may be unpredictable. If the costs and gains are evenly balanced, a threat is not worth the risk. If the value of the threat depends on its outcome and that is unpredictable, you confront a more difficult decision. If you are a risk taker, you may want to proceed. If not, you should eschew threats in this circumstance.

GENERAL RULES

Although there is no right answer for everyone, there are some general rules that ought to govern consideration of threats:

1. *Do not make threats that promise only marginal gains.* They are not worth the effort or possible negative repercussions. They can anger their target and make any agreement impossible. Use threats to make marginal gains only when there are readily available alternatives and you have no relationship to preserve.
2. *Do not make threats where the costs of failure would be greater than the benefits of success.* If the outcome of the threat is unpredictable, the odds are against you. A threat is only worth the risk if you are reasonably confident that it will succeed.
3. *Do not make threats you are unprepared to carry out.* For reasons that Chapters 12 and 13 make clear, bargainers frequently miscalculate the consequences of their threats. Threats that seem credible and sufficient to the party making them may not appear that way to their targets. If the costs of backing away from or carrying out your threat are greater than the cost of accepting the other side's final offer, you should do the latter.
4. *Do not make threats likely to damage important relationships.* Even when successful, such threats may bring short-term gains at the expense of greater long-term losses.
5. *Threats are best used to prevent loss.* They can effectively communicate that the other side's terms are not in your interest. If the threat works, it can help you obtain a favorable outcome. If not, you are still better off than you would be with terms the other side offered or was prepared to accept.
6. *Threats can be used to limit another's gains.* If the other side is pushing for very advantageous terms, you may be able to use a threat to negotiate for more moderate terms that it will still regard as advantageous. Negotiations about excess value—what's left after both sides meet their minimum requirements—often turn on resolve. A threat not to settle, if credible, can confer a decisive advantage.

Communicating Threats

Threats can be blunt and definite. One lawyer tells another: "This is my client's final offer. Take it or leave it." Threats can also be tentative and ambiguous. The lawyer might have said: "I don't think we're getting anywhere in this negotiation." This statement also communicates dissatisfaction, but it leaves open the possibility of further bargaining. It could be construed by the other side as an invitation to make another offer.

A clear and definite threat is less likely to be misunderstood. It is also more likely to be taken seriously because it does not hedge. For this reason, you will lose face and credibility if the other side rejects your offer and you fail to carry out your threat. Clear and definite threats are also more likely to arouse anger. After all, nobody likes being served with an ultimatum.

Tentative and ambiguous threats are less likely to provoke. If they fail to elicit the desired concessions, you can continue to bargain with minimal loss of face or credibility. They convey a sense of urgency but not of finality. They can be a precursor to more definitive threats.

What kind of threat should you make? It generally makes sense to start with tentative and ambiguous threats; they can be used to break an impasse. If the other side does not get the hint or refuses to budge, you can make a more definitive threat of nonsettlement. Such a threat needs to be precise and credible.

To be precise, you need to communicate as clearly as possible the terms you are willing (or unwilling) to accept and your intention to terminate the negotiation (and go to court, or take whatever other action might be relevant) if the other side still rejects those terms. In some circumstances, you will want to impose a time limit.

To be credible, you must convince the other side that you are going to carry out your threat. This can be as simple as putting your wallet back in your pocket and making a move toward the door. When your freedom to say no is not so evident, you need to make convincing demonstrations of your ability to do without agreement. We have already looked at several ways this can be done. In most of these examples the bargainers made visible preparations to do without agreement (e.g., hired lawyers, put up for-sale signs, mobilized their armed forces) or began active pursuit of alternatives. A threat that is a bluff must appear to be very credible.

An alternative strategy for demonstrating credibility is to make a self-executing threat. This tactic is most appropriate when the costs of carrying out the threat are high. President Kennedy used this tactic in the Cuban missile crisis to impart credibility to his threat to attack Cuba unless the Soviet Union withdrew its missiles. Such threats are common in business. In August 1994, the owners of the Pittsburgh Pirates, exasperated with the team's deteriorating financial situation, invoked the escape clause in their contract, giving the mayor of Pittsburgh 180 days to find a buyer for the franchise or face its possible departure from the city. The threat was credible because other cities were keen to pick up a major league franchise.

The Consequences of Threats

If your threat succeeds, you have every reason to feel pleased. You got what you wanted by astutely exploiting the power imbalance between you and the other side. As a general rule, you should be magnanimous in victory and do what you can to make concession easier for the other side. Never gloat. Be appreciative of the concession and let the other side save face. If you can offer some minor concession in return, all the better.

If your threat fails, you still need to make some judgment about the other side's intent. Not every no is a real no. The other side might be bluffing, hoping that you were bluffing and that a show of firmness will elicit a concession, or it may be putting up a show of false resolve before caving in. It often pays to repeat your terms and give the other side a little more time to rethink its position before doing anything irrevocable. It is always possible that it will come around when faced with the certainty that the negotiation has failed. On the other hand, threats of nonsettlement can provoke counterthreats, of either nonsettlement or punishment.

Another possibility is partial success. The other side may accept your terms in principle but ask for some concession concerning them or another issue. If you will gain the substance of what you want, it is judicious to grant the other side's request and allow it to save face. If the proposed compromises are unacceptable, you can treat the other side's response as the opening offer in a renewed round of bargaining and make a counteroffer. Or, you can reject the other side's response as inadequate and see if it will give way.

Defusing Anger

Threats, especially threats of punishment, can transform a bargaining encounter into an unproductive test of wills. They can make the other side less pliable by bringing about a shift in its objectives from accommodation to proving that it cannot be coerced. This is a common problem in interpersonal bargaining, but it also affects diplomats and world leaders who should know better. We have already described Henry Kissinger's emotional response to Leonid Brezhnev's threat during the 1973 Middle East War.

What can be done to minimize emotional responses to threats? The first rule of thumb is to refrain from making threats in situations where they will be perceived as grossly inappropriate or as confirming evidence of your hostility. Two kinds of situations fit this bill. The first of these is where an amicable relationship exists and the other side expects to reach an accommodation through informal and friendly consultation. It would not be productive to threaten to unleash your pit bull against your neighbor's family if he refuses to lend you his lawn mower. The second is when relations are tense and the other side questions your motives and doubts your honesty. Like Brezhnev's threat, it is likely to be misunderstood and provoke an overreaction.

The response to threats is very much influenced by the tone and manner in which they are made. Telling the other side in a haughty voice, "This is my position; take it or leave it," can turn a bargaining encounter into a confrontation. Ultimatums risk a rupture, not only in the negotiation, but in the relationship.

Threats of nonsettlement can be put more softly than threats of punishment. The other side can be told: "I really sympathize with you and would like to reach an agreement, but this is the best offer I can make. Perhaps you can see your way clear to accepting it. If not, there is nothing more I can do." This statement conveys the same reluctance to make concessions but does so in a nonconfrontational way. It attempts to get the other side to see the bargaining from your perspective and to recognize that your interests, not your disposition, constrain you from making a concession. It always helps to explain your interests and constraints. If the other side accepts them as legitimate it is less likely to get angry, and should it become angered, that anger may be directed against the parties or constraints that limit your freedom of action.

Psychological experiments have identified a human bias in information processing known as the "fundamental attribution error." When people explain their own undesirable behavior, they tend to exaggerate the extent to which it was a response to situational constraints. When they are explaining negative behavior directed toward them, they are likely to attribute the behavior to the other person's disposition. The fundamental attribution error suggests that people whose demands you reject will be insensitive to any constraints that influenced your response. They are likely instead to exaggerate your freedom of choice and attribute your rejection to your unsympathetic, selfish, or aggressive nature. They then may become angry, with the consequences that we have described. The fundamental attribution error makes it all the more imperative for you to explain your decisions and try to make the other side understand why you have spurned their demands.

Responding to Threats

To this point in our analysis, we have assumed that you are making or contemplating threats. But you are just as likely to be the target of threats. How should you respond?

First of all, keep calm. Try not to get angry and try not to show any emotional response. Concentrate on your interests and whatever course of action they dictate. Sometimes it is important to face down threats. When the appearance of weakness would invite further demands or a tougher stance in subsequent negotiations, demonstrations of resolve can be helpful, even if they reduce the likelihood of agreement. Counterthreats are generally unnecessary and provocative.

Demonstrations of resolve sometimes facilitate agreement, by compelling the other side to reformulate its estimate of your character or interests. More often, threats and counterthreats make agreement more difficult, by increasing the cost of concession. If agreement is important, you will want to keep the negotiations on track and not let them (or you) be derailed by the other side's threat.

There are several productive ways to cope with threats. You can refuse to take them seriously. Try brushing the threat aside and telling the other side that it is inappropriate, that you will not respond to it and are going to pretend that it was never made, that you want to continue bargaining. You are in effect offering the other side an incentive and a face saving way to back away from a threat that it might have made incautiously.

Another tactic is to give the appearance of giving in to the demands, in order to keep the bargaining alive. Say that you accept the terms and are willing to reach an accommodation on that basis, but then impose conditions that undercut those terms or raise new demands. If the other side takes the bait and responds to your demands, you have succeeded in deflecting its threat and keeping the negotiation alive. If not, you have probably lost nothing in the process.

If both of these tactics fail, you will be forced to make a starker choice. You can accept or reject the other side's terms, or you can make counterthreats.

It is probably in your interest to accept the other side's terms when agreement is important to you and those terms still allow you to meet your minimum bargaining objectives. Unless the issue of resolve is paramount, the other side's threat should not deter you from making an agreement that is in your interest. You can still try to win marginally better terms by accepting the other side's offer with the proviso that it make this or that minor concession to you. To the extent that the other side is meeting its objectives, and is perhaps elated that its threat has succeeded, it may be prepared to make some concessions for the sake of agreement.

If the other side's threat is unacceptable or its terms are contrary to your interests, you should walk away from the table. In this situation, too, it is best to avoid displays of emotion. You may want or need to deal with the party again. A simple, clear explanation of why you will not give in to a threat or accept terms that are not in your interests should suffice.

Counterthreats are appropriate to only a narrow range of situations. When you think the threat is a bluff, a counterthreat to terminate the negotiations can sometimes get the other side to back down and resume bargaining. The important thing in this circumstance is to let the other side save face. This can be done by making your counterthreat and then offering to withdraw it if the other side does the same. You might say: "Look, you can't intimidate me. Threats are not going to get either of us anywhere. Why don't we forget about them and see if we have the basis for a mutually advantageous agreement."

Threats sometimes have implications that extend beyond the issues on the table. If the other side's threat seems inappropriate to the context or relationship, it may indicate a very different understanding of that context or relationship. If so, it is in your interest to see if you can reach a common understanding. A better mutual understanding may lead the other side to withdraw its threat. Chapter 12 examines this strategy in detail. Alternatively, you may want to reassess the value of negotiation. If the other side's understanding of the situation or of the relationship is very different from yours, any agreement may be difficult to implement.

Sometimes, threats made against you are really aimed at third parties. In the late 1950s and early 1960s, Soviet and Chinese leaders made numerous threats against the United States. In a well-publicized speech, Mao Tse-tung called upon the peoples of the Third World to rise up and overthrow American imperialism. Speeches like these convinced many American officials that communist China was entering a more aggressive and dangerous phase in its foreign policy. We know today that the root cause of many of these polemics was the growing tension between China and the Soviet Union. Leaders on both sides were outbidding each other in their expressions of hostility toward the capitalist West in an attempt to win the support of other communist parties.

The reverse phenomenon also occurs: targets of threats can incorrectly dismiss them as really directed against third parties. In October 1973, Leonid Brezhnev had threatened to send Soviet forces to Egypt if the Nixon administration did not agree to joint intervention. The United States responded with a DefCon III strategic nuclear alert. The Soviet Politburo was unaware of Brezhnev's threat, and most of its members viewed the American nuclear alert as a totally disproportionate response to any differences that might have developed between their two countries during the course of the Middle East War. They incorrectly attributed the alert to President Nixon's political need to distract public opinion from the Watergate scandal.

These international examples have domestic analogues. Threats in business and personal disputes are also sometimes intended to impress other parties (e.g., business associates, other companies, spouses). Before responding to a threat, ask yourself whether you are in fact the target, and if so, why? If you think the threat is really aimed at someone else, you need to decide if it is in your interest to reply. In many circumstances it may be wise to ignore the threat and continue bargaining as if it had never been made.

Chapter 9

How to Gain Leverage

Asymmetries confer bargaining advantages. They shape impressions of what an agreement ought to look like. Based on its reading of the context, each side estimates how much it can demand and how much it must give up to reach an accommodation. Asymmetries provide the basis for both the strategy of rewards and the strategy of punishment. Crosscutting asymmetries make it possible for one or both sides to make low-cost concessions. Reinforcing asymmetries permit the side that benefits from them to make threats of nonsettlement or punishment.

The preceding chapters treated asymmetries as given, but bargainers often have it in their power to create asymmetries or reshape existing ones. Perceptions of asymmetries, as distinct from the asymmetries themselves, can also be manipulated to gain advantage.

Creating and Restructuring Asymmetries

Within the constraints imposed by context, resources, and imagination, any asymmetry can be created or altered. For purposes of illustration, we will look at how this can be done with three asymmetries: resources, alternatives, and time.

Resources

Powerful bargainers control many resources. But resources in and of themselves rarely confer bargaining advantages. They need to be exploited if you want to create or reinforce other asymmetries. When American air traffic controllers went on strike in 1981, they intended to bring air traffic to a complete halt and thereby generate enormous pressure on the government to end the strike by acceding to their demands. However, the Reagan administration convinced the federal courts to declare the strike illegal and instructed the Federal Aviation Administration to fire the controllers and train new ones for their places. Independent experts maintained that the quality of air traffic control would decline, but the Reagan administration persevered, defeated the strike and sent a powerful cautionary message to other unions. The administration in effect used its power to deprive the union of any of the bargaining advantages that it had expected to gain from a strike.

Weaker parties frequently seek outside support to redress a power imbalance. The largely itinerant grape pickers of California had fought unsuccessfully to compel the growers to recognize and bargain with their union. They succeeded when their leader, Cesar Chavez, mobilized the support of more powerful unions and prominent Hollywood personalities behind a nationwide grape boycott.

Another strategy is to deprive the other side of its resources or their bargaining value. In the 1960s, a colleague of mine living in New York City divorced a woman whose father was a senior partner in a major New York law firm. The father-in-law dragged him through the courts, stuck him with alimony payments, and had his salary garnisheed when he refused to pay on the grounds that his ex-wife was capable of supporting herself. The ex-husband struck back by finding a new job, still in New York, and opening a checking account in Washington, D.C., where a friend took his telephone messages. He gradually convinced his ex-wife that he had moved out of state. The father-in-law had the alimony judgment entered in federal court and served on the company in Washington where my friend had dropped hints he was working. The company insisted that they had no one by that name on their payroll. My friend then offered to pay $100 more per month in child support if his ex-wife would drop her claims to alimony. The irate father-in-law spurned the offer but pursued his quest for alimony no further when his daughter began to receive the additional payments.

Sometimes, both parties try to augment their resources while depriving the other side of its. In the former Yugoslavia, Bosnian Serbs sought to occupy as much of Bosnia as they could and to kill and expel non-Serbs from captured territory. They blockaded Bosnian cities to deny their inhabitants the food and munitions they needed to carry on the struggle. In retaliation, the Western powers instituted a blockade of the rump Yugoslavia, to destroy its economy and encourage its leaders to restrain the Bosnian Serb forces. Bosnians have also sought arms from Middle Eastern countries to facilitate their recapture of lost territory. Armenians and Azerbaijanis resorted to similar tactics in their struggle for control of Nagorno-Karabakh. Armenians drew money and supplies from the Armenian diaspora and gained the upper hand militarily. Azerbaijanis responded with a blockade of Armenia, to deprive it of the food and military supplies it received from Russia, and attempted to forge a defensive alliance with Turkey.

Alternatives

Bargainers develop alternatives as a hedge against failure, but viable alternatives also confer significant bargaining advantages. In the 1950s, following bad harvests elsewhere in Latin America, Colombia sought major increases in the price of its coffee beans. American coffee companies, the major purchasers of Colombian coffee, responded by developing the technology to produce instant coffee. By the end of the decade, instant coffee had swept the American market and made purchasers less dependent on yearly production and less vulnerable to attempts by growers to raise prices in years when harvests were poor.

Alternatives can be a critical determinant of price. Air travel is a case in point. It costs twice as much to fly the 200-odd miles from Ithaca to New York City than the 2,500 miles from New York to Los Angeles. There is no competition between Ithaca and New York, a consequence of deregulation. The same is true on the Pittsburgh-Chicago route, where an unrestricted midweek fare is $450. It is only $99 from Cleveland to Chicago, where two airlines compete for passengers. USAir, which has a monopoly between Pittsburgh and Chicago, has been accused of using its influence with Allegheny County authorities to keep other airlines from flying this and other lucrative routes. Consumer groups have organized to pressure local authorities to free up gates at Pittsburgh International Airport for competitors. If they succeed, prices will drop.

Time

Bargainers who believe that time is in their favor may try to postpone or stall negotiations. We have already told the story of Thermistocles who dragged out his negotiations with Sparta until he received word that the defensive walls around Athens had been completed. Bargainers who think time works against them will try to conclude negotiations as quickly as possible. They may use threats or rewards toward this end. Last year, my youngest son offered to contribute ten dollars of his own money toward the purchase of roller blades if my wife would drive him to the mall that very day to buy them. Entering into the spirit of the negotiations, she insisted on fifteen dollars. They finally agreed on ten, if David came up with the cash and cleaned his room before they set foot in the car.

Not infrequently, both sides try to control time, one to gain an advantage, the other to deny it. Khrushchev ordered missiles sent and deployed secretly in Cuba. He reasoned that Kennedy would be more likely to accept them if the missiles were operational and armed with nuclear warheads. When American intelligence discovered the missile sites, Kennedy kept the knowledge secret for a week so he could formulate and prepare a response. After Kennedy announced a naval quarantine of Cuba, Khrushchev ordered Soviet ships not to challenge the blockade and attempted to draw out the crisis in the hope that Soviet construction crews, working around the clock, could ready the missile sites and deter an American attack. Kennedy responded by giving Khrushchev a de facto ultimatum: he had Robert Kennedy tell Soviet ambassador Anatoliy Dobrynin that the pressures to attack were mounting and that military action against Cuba could probably not be postponed for more than twenty-four hours. Khrushchev, who had by then extracted two important concessions from Kennedy, hastened to communicate his willingness to withdraw the missiles.

Pressure Points

Bargaining encounters sometimes turn on the ability of one side to exploit a weakness of the other. During the Cold War, Hong Kong and Berlin were vulnerable cities. They could not have been defended from attack by the Chinese or Soviets, respectively, and they were dependent on adjacent communist governments for their fuel and food. At various times in the 1950s, the People's Republic of China threatened to shut off Hong Kong's water supply, to extract political concessions from Britain. In 1948–49, Joseph Stalin imposed a blockade of Berlin to prevent unification of the three Western-occupied zones of Germany. The Western powers organized an airlift to supply the city with food and fuel, and Stalin, unwilling to go to war, sought an accommodation. In the late 1950s and early

1960s Nikita Khrushchev, hoping to compel the West to recognize East Germany, tried and failed to exploit Berlin's vulnerability. Khrushchev told his advisors: "Berlin is the West's balls. Whenever I want them to scream, I just squeeze."

Hong Kong and Berlin were preexisting pressure points. Occasionally, a pressure point can be developed during the course of bargaining and be effectively exploited. The Greek historian Thucydides describes an Athenian expedition to Pylos during the stalemated Peloponnesian War. The Spartan defenders made a tactical error, became trapped at the headland of a peninsula, and were forced to surrender. Among the prisoners were 120 sons of Sparta's leading families; their capture compelled Sparta to sue for peace to get them back. Modern-day terrorists also resort to kidnapping; they take hostages in planes, ships, or schools and threaten to kill them unless their demands are met. The Hezbollah successfully used hostage Israeli airmen to gain the release of more than a hundred Shi'ite prisoners held by Israel.

Manipulating Asymmetries

Asymmetries are subjective. They have no meaning other than that imposed on them by the bargainers. This makes it possible for either side to manipulate the other's understanding of any asymmetry. People being sued routinely try to mislead plaintiffs or their attorneys about the extent of their resources or their accessibility. By hiding or shielding assets, they hope to convince the other side to settle for less. People facing negotiation deadlines often try to hide the fact, to keep from being exploited by the other side, or even try to convey the impression that they have all the time in the world. Bargainers also sometimes invent phony constituencies that they claim are constraining them from making concessions they would otherwise grant.

The impression of advantage can confer real advantage. Job candidates are more likely to extract favorable terms from prospective employers if they can convince the employer that they have other job offers. And a company can attempt to hire someone for less by making a case that there are other highly qualified people eager to take the job. A law suit may be settled for less if the plaintiff believes that collecting the judgment would be extremely difficult even if it won the case.

Impressions of advantages can sometimes be constructed out of thin air. A colleague of mine recently went shopping for a giant-screen television set. He was offered a good price, $800, on a floor model at a discount appliance store. He immediately went to another well-known appliance store that advertises that it will not be undersold. It was offering the same model for $875. He said to the salesman, "What if I told you that I could get it for $750?" This was $50 less than the price he had been quoted, and he neglected to report that it was for a set that was no longer new. The salesman hemmed and hawed but finally agreed to lower his price to $750. In a display of real chutzpah, my colleague asked in an indignant voice why he should buy the set here for the same price. What was in it for him? The salesman, speechless at first, agreed to come down another $25. This determined bargainer paid the $725 and left the store with a new television and a big smile.

Elaborate ruses have been used to gain bargaining advantages. Hitler and Luftwaffe chief Hermann Goering made far-reaching claims for the German air force, inflating several fold its number of operational aircraft. The Luftwaffe conducted air shows to impress influential foreigners with its capability. American air hero and isolationist Charles A. Lindbergh, flattered and entertained by Hitler and Goering, went to London to convince British leaders that their cities would be destroyed in a war with Germany. British concern for their vulnerable cities contributed to the Chamberlain government's decision to appease Hitler.

In the 1950s, the Soviets repeatedly tried to give the impression of strategic superiority. At the 1955 May Day celebration, the Soviet air force repeatedly flew the same bomber squadrons over Red Square convincing a surprisingly gullible American military delegation that they had thousands of long-range bombers. Following the success of the first Sputniks in 1957, Nikita Khrushchev made great claims about Soviet rocketry and its ability to destroy cities in Western Europe and the United States. Khrushchev's strategic boasts triggered the famous "missile gap" that was not exposed until American satellite reconnaissance of the Soviet Union in 1961 revealed a substantial American lead in missiles. Khrushchev attempted to exploit his putative strategic advantage to browbeat the West into making concessions on Berlin. He failed, because Western leaders were fearful that any concessions would lead to further gains.

As these examples indicate, bargainers can claim advantages they do not possess or hide weaknesses that work to their disadvantage. Experienced bargainers take nothing that others say or do at face value, because they expect bargainers to exaggerate their advantages and downplay their weaknesses. Whenever possible, they seek independent confirmation. Like the IRS dealing with a taxpayer, they discount, or convey the impression that they discount, any claim not backed by compelling evidence.

Given the subjective nature of asymmetries and the practice of misleading opponents, legitimate efforts to enlighten others about your strengths or the constraints you face risk being misconstrued as misinformation. On several occasions at Yalta, Franklin Roosevelt rejected Stalin's demands for a free hand in Poland on the grounds that allies or domestic ethnic constituencies would not approve. Irked by this tactic, the Soviet dictator urged Roosevelt to "carry out better propaganda" among Polish-American voters to bring them in line. At their next session, Stalin invoked the same defense to reject one of Roosevelt's demands. He insisted, quite falsely, that he was willing to go along with the president but that Ukrainians and Byelorussians would never agree!

Exploiting Weakness

Credible threats are usually based on favorable asymmetries. Sometimes, unfavorable asymmetries can be exploited just as effectively. To do this, the side making the threat must be able to demonstrate that failure to meet its demands would also prove costly to the other side.

Mexico's negotiations with the United States over debt refinancing offer a good illustration of how weakness can be exploited successfully. Mexico's mounting debt was the result of deficit spending, borrowing abroad to finance this spending, and more borrowing to service the interest on the earlier loans. By 1982, the Mexican economy was on the verge of collapse, and its government sought relief from the United States, its principal creditor.

Mexico's desperate state and financial dependence on the United States should have made it relatively easy for Washington to dictate terms, but President Lopez Portillo turned his country's weakness into a powerful bargaining asset. Mexican default would have been catastrophic for Mexico, but it would also have been extremely costly for the United States. American banks held 30 percent of Mexico's external debt, a sum equal to 46 percent of the capital of the seventeen largest American banks. If Mexico defaulted, American banks would lose their loans, triggering a banking crisis, and many American companies would suffer serious losses from the resulting decline in trade between the two countries. The $14 billion Mexican citizens had on deposit in American banks and the $30 billion they owned in American real estate provided additional reasons for Washington to reach an accommodation with their government. An economic collapse would also have had profoundly negative political consequences for the United States because it would have strengthened the appeal of anti-American, left-wing political forces in Mexico. By playing on the expected consequences of default, Portillo was able to convince the Reagan administration to refinance Mexico's debt at very favorable terms.

In a variant of this strategy, the bargainer attempts to transform weakness into strength by portraying itself as indispensable. In the 1950s and early 1960s the United States tried unsuccessfully to push South Vietnam's dictator Ngo Dinh Diem into land and political reform. Dependent on the United States for economic aid and military assistance, Diem was nevertheless in a strong position as long as Washington could find no alternative leader and feared that his weakness or overthrow would facilitate a communist takeover. Secretary of State Dean Rusk agreed with his critics that Diem was a "bastard," but insisted "he's the only one we've got." Arabs and Israelis have also played this game. Yasir Arafat insisted that the United States and Israel deal with him and the Palestine Liberation Organization because other Palestinian factions were more extreme. Following the Israeli Labor Party's victory in 1992, Yitzhak Rabin made the same claim, warning the United States, Syria, and the Palestinians that failure to reach an accommodation would bring the right-wing Likud back to power. Mutual fears of the alternative provided a strong incentive for Israelis and Palestinians to begin talking to each other.

The strategy of weakness has been used with equal effect in personal and business relations. It is the hallmark of passive-aggressive behavior. In a well-known "lightbulb joke," a Jewish mother tells her son: "It's all right dear; you don't have to change it. I'll just sit here in the dark." The son, racked by guilt, presumably rushes to the basement for a new bulb and step ladder. Princess Diana appears to have used the same strategy. By publicly disclosing her suicide attempts—and tacitly suggesting that she would try again because life with Charles had become so miserable—she confronted Queen Elizabeth with the prospect of serious scandal at a time when the royal family was reeling from mounting criticism in Parliament and the press. The queen quickly reached a financial settlement with Diana.

Threats of corporate suicide can also shake loose concessions. The decline of the American automobile industry had damaging consequences for the American economy as a whole. This was repeatedly exploited by automobile executives to obtain favorable loans and relief from various safety and fuel-economy measures. Industry representatives convinced governmental agencies and the Congress, rightly or wrongly, that the alternative was greater losses and more unemployment.

When threats rest on favorable asymmetries, the side making them attempts to convince the other that it will suffer proportionately more from the consequences of nonsettlement. The opposite is true for threats based on unfavorable asymmetries; the party making the threat will suffer more. Such threats can still succeed if they meet three conditions:

1. *The threats must raise the prospect of significant loss for their target.* This was a distinguishing feature of all of our examples. Each of the targets recognized that it would suffer considerable political, economic, or psychological loss if it imposed too stringent conditions on the other side.

2. *The targets of the threats must be more concerned with absolute than relative loss.* When bargainers are motivated by relative gain, threats against them will fail, no matter how costly the consequences, if the side making the threat will lose more. Airlines routinely engage in price wars and governments in wars of attrition. They recognize how costly these contests are but expect their adversaries to suffer even more from them. They also expect long-term benefits from the contest that will more than compensate them for their short-term losses.

   The more concerned the target is with avoiding absolute loss, the more effective will be threats against it by weaker or otherwise disadvantaged parties. Nikita Khrushchev exploited this situation during the Cuban missile crisis. He threatened to ignore the American blockade of Cuba even though the Soviet Union lacked the forces to mount any kind of naval challenge in the Caribbean. If a conventional war began, it could have rapidly escalated to a nuclear conflict. Here, too, the Soviet Union was at a significant disadvantage. General Curtis Le May, head of the Strategic Air Command (SAC), had advised President Kennedy that SAC could destroy the Soviet Union with the loss of no more than three American cities. Kennedy was appalled by Le May's nonchalance. Throughout the crisis, the president's closest advisors have reported, he was committed to avoiding escalation, even though he recognized his country's overwhelming military superiority. His concern for absolute loss led him to make a series of concessions to Khrushchev.

3. *The threats must be credible.* As we noted in the previous chapter, it is

difficult to make believable threats when you will suffer proportionately more from carrying them out. Such threats can sometimes be made credible if the side making them is emotionally aroused and thus appears more likely to do something irrational. Princess Diana's threats may have succeeded for this reason. Another way to make suicidal threats more credible is to link them to a principle that transcends narrow calculations of self-interest. People willing to die for their religion or nation have sometimes forced more powerful adversaries to make concessions. The Irish, Vietnamese, and Afghans have used this tactic with success.

You can also try to give costly threats an autonomous probability. The threat of economic chaos used by Mexican president Portillo in his negotiations with the Reagan administration did not require any implementation. There was little or nothing Portillo could do to prevent chaos if the United States did not agree to roll over Mexico's debt. This was also true of the political threats made by Diem, Arafat, and Rabin. They would have been carried out by other parties, whom the leaders in question were powerless to control.

Every strategy has a drawback. Bargainers who base threats on weakness can get themselves into serious trouble if their threats are insufficient or incredible. They may have to back down, with all the loss of face and bargaining reputation that this entails. Worse still, they may have to carry out their threats. The self-immolation of David Koresh and his followers was the result of their failure to convince either the Bureau of Alcohol, Tobacco, and Firearms or the Federal Bureau of Investigation to take seriously their threat of mass suicide. In the case of threats that have an autonomous probability, both their maker and their target may have to watch helplessly as the worst-case scenario unfolds.

The Importance of Information

Our analysis of asymmetries points to the critical role of information. It can help a bargainer develop an asymmetry or deny it to the other side. Kennedy exploited American intelligence's discovery of Soviet missile site construction in Cuba to do both. Information can also help a bargainer manipulate another actor's understanding of an asymmetry. The market woman who knows the average selling price of mangoes may be able to convince the ignorant tourist that they sell for twice as much. The market analyst who knows that demand for a given product will increase may be able to negotiate a contract at a low price from a supplier who is not so well informed.

Lack of information, or even the appearance of ignorance, makes a bargainer vulnerable to exploitation. Studies indicate that women are quoted higher prices than men for similar automobiles because salesmen assume they know less about cars and less about negotiation. Salesmen can be taken for a ride when they are ill informed, as was the television salesman in our example. The same is true of diplomats. In negotiating the Open Door policy toward China, President Theodore Roosevelt obtained the concurrence of all the major European powers by telling each of them that the others had already agreed.

Information is an asymmetry in its own right. Nothing illustrates this better than collective bargaining in major league baseball. In 1985, management persuaded the players' union to extend salary arbitration on the grounds of financial hardship. Subsequent studies of the industry revealed that management had misrepresented the situation; income for 1986–89 was $500 million more each year than estimated. Between 1983 and 1985, player payrolls represented 50–53 percent of total industry revenues. By 1988 they had dropped to 46 percent. With this information in hand, the union entered the 1989 negotiations with their eyes open, unprepared to trust management figures or forecasts. After hard bargaining that continued into Spring Training, an agreement was reached that guaranteed players 48 percent of revenues as well as concessions on other important issues. First for management, then for the players, access to information about profits and salaries was the key to successful bargaining.

Experienced bargainers make it their business to obtain as much information as possible beforehand and to continue their search for relevant information as bargaining continues. When possible, they also attempt to control the information available to other parties, providing or withholding information about preferences, asymmetries, and context as it suits their needs.

From Theory to Practice

Asymmetries are critical to bargaining. They determine the range of feasible bargaining goals and the efficacy of the strategies used to achieve them. The more favorable the asymmetries, the better the terms you can demand. Favorable asymmetries also facilitate successful use of the strategies of rewards and punishment. For both these reasons, it is imperative that you understand the nature and extent of the asymmetries in any bargaining situation.

In many bargaining encounters, there is little or nothing you can do in the short term to restructure the context. You must work with the asymmetries already present and make the best of the situation. However, with a little forethought and effort, you may be able to alter the context to your advantage. The checklist below has been prepared with this end in mind.

1. *Identify all the relevant asymmetries.* These asymmetries (need to settle, resources, alternatives, time, precedent, reputation, interests, and willingness to suffer) are described in Chapter 8. Do any of these asymmetries favor you? Which ones favor the other side? Which asymmetries are most pronounced, and whom do they favor? Mapping the asymmetries in this manner should give you a reasonable idea of the power balance.

2. *What can be done to strengthen your bargaining position?* This can be accomplished in two ways: new asymmetries can be created or existing ones shifted further in your favor. The possibilities of doing either will obviously vary from situation to situation and from one asymmetry to another:

Need to settle. People need to settle because they have no attractive alternatives. What can you do to increase your alternatives or limit those of the other side? Given the nature of what is at stake, what level of resources is it worthwhile to invest in this effort?

Resources. People generally have more resources than they realize. What resources (e.g., time, money, contacts, access to information or expert advice) do you have? How could these resources be used to create new asymmetries or shift existing ones further in your favor?

Alternatives. Alternatives are almost always worth exploring and sometimes worth developing. The existence of a viable alternative lets you face the prospect of nonsettlement with equanimity. The most obvious alternative is a fresh negotiation with someone else for more or less the same end (i.e., if this person won't come down in price on her '92 van, I'll try answering another ad). Another possibility is to reconsider the end itself (i.e., used cars are too expensive, maybe I can use public transportation and the occasional taxi). What choices are open to you? What can you do in the short term to explore or develop them?

Time. Would time pressure on the other side be to your advantage? If so, what can you do to create or intensify it? Can you impose a deadline? Can you make that deadline credible? If time pressure constrains the other side from making concessions, what can you do to alleviate it or its consequences?

Precedent. Will agreement have implications for subsequent negotiations? If so, will concessions be more costly for the other side? Is there anything you can do to limit the precedent-setting nature of the negotiation? Would it make sense to talk to the other side about the problem and together find some way to protect that side from the expected negative consequences of concession? Alternatively, can you make it more difficult for the other side to extract concessions, by linking this negotiation to others and emphasizing your need to avoid setting a costly precedent?

Reputation. You can strengthen your bargaining position by making a credible claim that your reputation is on the line. To do this, you need to show how your performance will set a precedent or is being monitored by important third parties. Do you have a spouse, business partner, or boss you can exploit for this purpose?

Interests. The more you have at stake, the more convincing your claim to reject an unfavorable settlement. But if you have a lot at stake, threats of nonsettlement are only credible if you have alternatives. To develop this asymmetry, you need to demonstrate the extent to which your major interests are on the line and will be adversely affected by an unsatisfactory outcome. You also need to convince the other side that you have other options and therefore feel free to walk away from a disadvantageous offer.

Willingness to suffer. People are generally more willing to suffer for their principles than for their interests. To exploit this asymmetry, you need to link your demands to broader notions of justice or self-esteem. The tactic will be most effective when the other side recognizes the legitimacy of the principles you invoke.

3. *What can be done to reduce the other side's advantages?* Suppose, for example, that time is working to the other side's advantage because

you have a known deadline. You could undercut this advantage if you could extend or escape the deadline. In a court case, you might come up with reasonable grounds with which to convince the judge to grant a continuance. If the other side has more resources, you might borrow or draw on resources of associates or friends.

As a general rule, the best way to limit the other side's advantages is to reduce your vulnerabilities. On occasion, another's advantages can be attacked directly. In business and politics, bargainers routinely try to wean away the other side's allies or otherwise weaken its coalition, deprive it of constituency support, create diversions that drain its attention or resources, or restructure the rules of bargaining. The last of these approaches was favored by the striking baseball players when they went to court to get an injunction and sought to drum up support in Congress for depriving baseball owners of their longstanding exemption from antitrust legislation. You have to ask yourself what tactics are appropriate to your situation.

If the other side is clever, it will also seek to maximize its advantages by creating new asymmetries or further shifting those already in its favor. To forestall this, you need to pay some attention to potential asymmetries. Could the other side use its resources to create a new advantage for itself? What asymmetries is it likely to try to create or strengthen? What can you do to protect yourself against this?

Bargaining asymmetries are a means to an end. They may help you extract concessions from the other side and get a better agreement. But it often takes time and resources to structure and communicate bargaining advantages. You need to weigh these costs against any possible gain. The nature and importance of your interests should determine the efforts and resources you are willing to expend in pursuit of bargaining advantage.

4. *Convince the other side of your advantages.* Having greater resources, more alternatives, and less need to settle does not automatically confer bargaining advantage. The other side must recognize those asymmetries and the extent to which they favor you. In some bargaining encounters, your advantages may be obvious. In others, they are not so apparent.

Even when you think advantages are obvious, they may not be. The other side may have a different understanding of the context. It may not grasp your advantages (or disadvantages), or not think them germane, and may develop different expectations of what would constitute a reasonable agreement. People also perceive contexts differently because they are very committed to achieving their bargaining goals and are strongly motivated to see the context as conducive to those goals.

Different understandings of context occasionally abet the strategies of reward and punishments. In the late 1960s, the United States and the Soviet Union hastened to negotiate a treaty limiting deployment of antiballistic missile defenses because each superpower mistakenly thought the other was close to deploying a capable system. More often than not, different understandings of context confound bargaining strategies. Chapters 11 and 12 examine this problem in detail and describe what can be done to bring about a common understanding of asymmetries relevant to the bargaining.

5. *Consider trying to create the impression of bargaining advantage.* This can take two forms: asymmetries in your favor that justify better terms or weaknesses in the form of constraints that make concessions more costly. "Impression management" is an art that requires imagination and some acting skill. You need to find an asymmetry that is important and amenable to manipulation, and you need to convince the other side of your putative advantage or constraints. This may require nothing more than a good story, as it did for my colleague buying a television. But it sometimes involves considerable effort and preparation, as did my other colleague's attempt to convince his former wife and father-in-law that he had moved to Washington.

Playing fast and loose with reality can be a risky business. If caught and exposed, your personal and bargaining reputation can suffer with all the negative consequences that entails. Creating false impressions of advantage is most appropriate in isolated, one-time bargaining encounters in which no precedent will be set and no relationship is on the line. This was the situation in which my colleague shopping for a television found himself. It may also be worth the risk when the stakes are high. It was the fear of great financial loss that drove the ex-husband in the alimony case.

6. *Consider exploiting your weaknesses.* When it is impossible to create bargaining asymmetries in your favor, or the impression that they are in your favor, you need to establish modest bargaining goals. Exploiting your weaknesses can get you better terms.

Earlier in the chapter, we argued that weakness can be exploited successfully when the other side is concerned with absolute versus relative gains, your threat raises the prospect of significant loss, and your threat is fully credible. If these conditions are present, or can be met, you should consider making a threat of nonsettlement.

Beyond meeting these three conditions, the key to success is to frame reasonable demands. Given the cost to you of a breakdown in negotiations, you want to maximize your chances of settlement. Outrageous demands are more likely to be dismissed by the other side, putting you in the position of having to back down or carry out a threat that, while costly to the other side, is by definition more costly still to you. In framing your demands, look for some precedent or principle that can justify them. Alternatively, explain your need for concessions to placate a critical constituency.

You also need to make sure that the other side has a good, or better yet an exaggerated, appreciation of what it will lose in the absence of an agreement. In the Mexican debt renegotiation, President Reagan was apprised of the facts of the case by a fully credible source—his own treasury department. Sometimes, the side employing the strategy has to enlighten the target of its threat about what it stands to lose. Such efforts should be accompanied by attempts to stress the advantages that will accrue to both sides from accommodation.

Part 3 A Bargain Is Just the Beginning

Chapter 10

Ratification

Bargaining does not always end with agreement. To ratify and implement the agreement, one or both sides may have to gain the support of third parties. Failure to do so may render the agreement worthless. In 1919, Woodrow Wilson went to the Paris Peace Conference to gain allied support for his dream of a League of Nations. He worked painstakingly to sell the League and made important concessions on territorial and other issues to France and Italy in return for their support. Wilson made no similar effort to woo the Senate, and a coalition of miffed senators and ideological opponents subsequently voted to reject the Treaty of Versailles and American participation in the League. Contract negotiators and divorce lawyers encounter similar problems; unions, boards of directors, and clients sometimes reject agreements they have taken many hours to negotiate.

Critical third parties can influence agreements at three different stages of the bargaining process. They can intervene at the outset to try to prevent or shape an agreement. In the 1970s, West Coast lumbermen contended that importing cheaper, duty-free shakes and shingles from British Columbia would have a ruinous effect on the American lumber industry. They waged an active but unsuccessful campaign to exclude lumber from the free-trade negotiations then underway with Canada. Irish and Palestinian militants have used violence to try to derail negotiations. On several occasions when Northern Irish peace talks were about to begin, Catholic or Protestant extremists carried out atrocities to polarize public opinion and make accommodation more difficult. In 1993–94, following the agreement between Israel and the Palestinian Liberation Organization, extremists on both sides resorted to terrorism to try to sabotage the peace process.

Third parties can also intervene in the ratification process. Not all agreements require ratification, but many do, and some of them fail to achieve it. We have already noted the Senate's rejection of the Treaty of Versailles. Other agreements that failed to achieve ratification include the SALT II agreement; the 1988 Meech Lake Accord, designed to bring Quebec within the Canadian Constitution; and the 1992 Treaty of Maastricht on European economic integration, rejected in a referendum by the Danish voters. Many of the critics of Meech Lake and Maastricht were not opposed in principle to the agreements' objectives but wanted to compel their governments to renegotiate them to take into account special interests or concerns. The Danish opposition to Maastricht succeeded in its goal.

Lastly, third parties can intervene in the implementation stage. This tactic appeals to parties who were unable to prevent negotiations, influence their outcome, or deny ratification of the resulting agreement. Examples include widespread violation of Prohibition by "wets," attempts by diehard segregationists to block implementation of school desegregation agreements, work-to-rule actions by disgruntled unions, and the sometimes categorical refusal by anticommunist American dock workers during the Cold War to load grain on ships bound for the Soviet Union.

Influence by third parties may be direct or indirect. Senators, boards of directors, and union members may have a legally mandated role in the ratification process. Failing that, they may have influence with people who do. Special interests, experts, and spouses are often in this position, too. Terrorists and others with influence over critical constituencies seek to turn public opinion against agreements. Without public support, leaders will find ratification and implementation of any political settlement more difficult, if not impossible.

When the stakes are high, the losing party will take the contest into any arena in which it has a hope of winning. The losing side in a law suit routinely appeals the judgment in the hope of a reversal. Political leaders appeal directly to the people, over the heads of "obstructionist" legislatures; President Boris Yeltsin of Russia did this in a 1992 referendum, to gain stronger powers and new parliamentary elections. Special interests sometimes make "end runs" around the bureaucracies charged with their oversight. American, Delta, and United airlines appealed to Transportation Secretary Andrew Card to reject the 1992 USAir–British Airways agreement. When Card ignored them, they waged a national campaign against the merger. They benefited from the fact that it was an election year and that President George Bush, behind in the polls, was increasingly desperate. He concluded that support for the Big Three airlines would win more votes than support for USAir, especially in hotly contested states, and he instructed Secretary Card to reject the merger.

The Nature of the Opposition

Bargainers whose agreements must be ratified need to adopt tactics appropriate to the challenge they confront. The nature of the challenge will be determined by the power and goals of the groups who participate in the ratification process. Opponents to ratification may come in three types.

The *dominant third party* is an individual, group, or organization that has enough clout or authority to veto an agreement. For labor negotiators, this might be a powerful faction within the union that must vote any settlement up or down. For a president with a proposed treaty, it is likely to be the leadership of the Senate. Dominant constituencies can be cohesive or loose coalitions and can have strong or weak preferences on the agreement in question. It is generally easiest to deal with dominant constituencies that are divided and have weak preferences.

Multiple constituencies pose a different kind of problem. They are likely to have clashing interests and conflicting demands. None of them is powerful enough alone to be a dominant constituency, but in alliance with others they could block ratification. American and Canadian negotiators of the 1987 free-trade accord had to cope with myriad third parties. Diverse interest groups on both sides of the border mobilized to pressure their respective governments to move ahead or back away from free-trade negotiations. Regional governments also became involved. In Canada, the province of Quebec, hoping to export more hydroelectric power to New York and New England, lobbied for free trade, while industries and unions in Ontario, who feared American manufacturing competition, lobbied against it. Negotiators had to plot a careful course through a veritable minefield of special interests, many of whom contended that the outcome was a life or death issue for them.

Blackmail constituencies are a special kind of dominant constituency. They have the power to block ratification or implementation but have no direct interest in the agreement. They use their veto power to extract concessions on other issues that are important to them. In the movie *Casablanca,* Louis, the prefect of police, uses his authority over exit visas to extract money from men and sexual favors from women. The Meech Lake Accord was held hostage by a coalition of Native Americans, feminists, and representatives of regional interests, all of whom wanted concessions from Canada's federal government in return for their support. Following their capture of both houses of Congress in the 1994 elections, the new Republican majority threatened to block appointments unless President Clinton cooperated with their legislative program.

Coping with Constituencies

There are various tactics bargainers can use to deal with third parties who threaten to block ratification of their agreements. Generally speaking, these tactics try to satisfy some or all of the opponents' demands, convince them that the agreement is in their interests, or limit their ability to impede ratification. The choice of tactic should be determined by the nature of the ratification problem.

Co-option

Bargainers can involve critical third parties in the negotiations in the hope of winning their support for the agreement. This tactic is based on the reasonable expectation that people who participate in negotiations will develop a proprietary interest in the agreement that emerges if it embodies some of their key goals. Hands-on experience can also expose third parties to information that may encourage them to revise their view of the negotiation. Jimmy Carter involved as many senators as he could in the Panama Canal and SALT II negotiations, rotating them through the American delegations. Some senators initially opposed to one or both negotiations changed their position. When queried afterwards, they talked about their new understanding of Latin America or arms control and how American interests would be best served by agreements.

Co-option can also be practiced without direct participation in the negotiations by third parties. The bargainers can consult with the third parties beforehand to ascertain their preferences and try to shape an agreement that as far as possible meets those preferences. Third parties can subsequently be kept informed of the progress of the negotiations. This is preferable to direct involvement when the participation of third parties would for any reason make it more difficult to negotiate an agreement.

Co-option is most effective when you are dealing with a dominant constituency. If the constituency can be bought off by addressing its concerns, and if those concerns are not inconsistent with your interests and the purposes of the negotiation, this may be a reasonable price to pay for ratification. The alternative, trying to win support for an agreement after it has been negotiated, is usually more difficult; the constituency is likely to make more far-reaching demands that would require renegotiation of the agreement. Even if renegotiation were possible, the side seeking it would be put in a disadvantaged position. The other side could demand concessions just for sitting down at the table.

The approach of co-option can sometimes be used with multiple constituencies. Selected individuals or representatives of groups can be brought into the negotiation. By doing this you can build a majority coalition among the individuals or groups who have the most to gain from the agreement. Co-option should not be used with multiple constituencies whose preferences are so diverse that their presence at the table would turn the negotiating forum into a tower of Babel. It is also inappropriate with blackmail constituencies, who have no interest in co-option.

Fait Accompli

The very opposite of co-option is the attempt to keep troublesome third parties in the dark about the negotiations, or at least at arm's length from them, until after agreement is reached. The agreement is then sprung on them as a *fait accompli,* leaving them little time to organize an effective opposition. The bargainer thereby maintains freedom of action during the negotiation and hopes to triumph over a disorganized opposition during the ratification process.

Faits accomplis will almost inevitably antagonize third parties if the agreement has failed to take their needs or interests into account. Henry Kissinger negotiated the Paris Peace Accords behind the back of the Republic of Vietnam. Kissinger reasoned that Vietnamese president Nguyen Van Thieu would oppose any agreement and that it was best to keep him isolated. Thieu was predictably furious when he learned of the accord and insisted that Kissinger renegotiate the terms. Le Duc Tho, the North Vietnamese negotiator, refused. To break the stalemate, President Nixon ordered B-52s to pound Hanoi for a week. The 1972 "Christmas bombing" killed thousands of civilians, alienated America's European allies, and led to huge antiwar demonstrations at home. It brought North Vietnam back to the table, but the final agreement, reached in early January 1973, was, a few cosmetic changes aside, exactly the same in substance as the earlier agreement that Thieu had refused to sign. Slightly mollified by the bombing, Thieu, who had no good options, reluctantly put his signature on a separate version of the agreement that did not mention by name the Viet Cong's provisional revolutionary government.

The *fait accompli* gambit is most effective when dealing with divided multiple constituencies. It can also be used with effect against a blackmail constituency, if it deprives that opponent of the time and momentum needed to cobble together a powerful opposing coalition. As we observed in the case of the Vietnamese, *faits accomplis* are least likely to succeed against a unified dominant constituency. It may still be an appropriate tactic to use if that party is unalterably opposed to the purpose of the negotiations and would do its best to block or sabotage agreement if aware of or a participant in the negotiations. Bombing is another matter.

Sequencing

This tactic combines the *fait accompli* and co-option approaches. After negotiating each part of an agreement, the bargainer brings it to key third parties for approval. This procedure enables the bargainer to negotiate with them privately, but it addresses the issues of interest to the third parties and thereby increases the likelihood that they will support the final agreement. Professional negotiators often use this approach, because they find it easier to sell an agreement in stages. They benefit from the fact that clients who have signed off on most of an agreement are less likely to reject it out of hand because they are unhappy with one or more provisions negotiated late in the game. For this reason, negotiators sometimes save the provisions they know will be most difficult to sell for last.

Sequencing is a good tactic to use with a dominant constituency not fundamentally opposed to the goals of the negotiation. By consulting that constituency before and during the bargaining, bargainers can shape an agreement that satisfies some or all of the opponent's major concerns. Sequencing will not work with a blackmail constituency. With a multiple constituency it is often hard to implement because of the difficulty of consulting and coordinating positions with several parties having different interests.

Isolation

This tactic seeks to make ratification possible by limiting the power of the opposition. Bargainers who must deal with third parties who oppose their agreement can try to discredit their leadership or motives, mobilize other third parties against them, or foment conflict between them and other groups. Opponents of the Clinton health care plan used this tactic in reverse. They succeeded in killing the prospect of legislation by using all of these moves against the president and the coalition of groups supporting him.

Isolation is an appropriate tactic to use against a constituency that cannot be bought off or would cost too much to buy off. It works best if that constituency is relatively weak or vulnerable.

Divide and Rule

A time-honored way of dealing with an opposing coalition is to buy off some of its members and isolate the others. In the 1860s, Otto von Bismarck used this tactic successfully against the liberal opposition in the Prussian parliament. The liberals tried to blackmail Bismarck and the king into granting more power to the parliament by refusing to authorize credits for the army. Bismarck knew the liberals were desperate to achieve national unification because of the economic rewards they expected to reap from a large, unified state without internal trade barriers. He reasoned that many liberals might be willing to compromise their democratic principles for the sake of unification. Bismarck provoked a war with Denmark as the first step toward this goal. The striking success of Prussian arms split the liberal party, with a substantial number of its representatives agreeing to a face-saving constitutional compromise proposed by Bismarck.

Bismarck's approach worked because the liberal coalition was not cohesive and because he found an issue that exposed the coalition's underlying cleavages. Both conditions are essential to the success of the divide and rule tactic when it is used against dominant constituencies. With multiple constituencies the tactic can succeed when one or more of the relevant individuals or groups can be bought off at low cost and the remainder will be left isolated or more ineffective by virtue of their inability to muster a majority.

Threats

Bargainers can sometimes strengthen their hand by convincing third parties that the costs of opposition are too high. Threats of punishment are frequently used to this end. In 1967, Turkey prepared to invade Cyprus in case it became necessary to protect Turkish Cypriot communities under attack from the Greek Cypriot militia. Turkish president Ismet Inönü raised the threat of military action in the hope that it would prompt the United States and Britain to restrain Greek Cypriots. President Johnson responded as Inönü expected, and Greek Cypriots were compelled to accept a cease-fire and United Nations forces to police it. Johnson also put pressure on Turkey. He sent Undersecretary of State George Ball to Ankara to deliver a stiff ultimatum: if Turkey invaded Cyprus, Washington would terminate all military aid and do nothing to defend Turkey against the Soviet Union. Inönü welcomed the threat, which he used to convince militant generals that an invasion was not in Turkey's interest.

This tactic is most likely to succeed against a vulnerable constituency confronting an agreement that achieves at least some of its goals. In the case of Turkey, the cease-fire and United Nations observer force undercut any need for invasion. The United States also had real levers of influence against Turkey, which relied on Washington for aid and military protection. When these conditions are met, threats can be used with effect against dominant and blackmail constituencies.

Side Payments

Third parties can sometimes be bought off. In the SALT II negotiations, the Joint Chiefs of Staff were a dominant constituency because the Senate would not ratify an arms control treaty they opposed. To win over the chiefs, President Carter gave in to their demand for the MX intercontinental ballistic missile.

Side payments are the primary objective of blackmail constituencies, who seek concessions on issues unrelated to the bargaining. Side payments can also be made to placate dominant constituencies or to build coalitions among multiple constituencies. This latter use of side payments is common by governments that need to build coalitions in legislatures in order to gain office or pass legislation. In Israel, the tiny religious parties have traditionally given their support to either Labor or Likud in return for a free hand in religious matters.

Persuasion

Third parties oppose agreements contrary to their interests. Their opposition can sometimes be dampened or, less frequently, overcome, by providing third parties with information about the agreement and its implications. Free-trade supporters in Canada and the United States conducted a successful campaign to educate industries about the likely consequences of free trade. Many businesses had focused on their expected losses, that is, on the expected penetration of their domestic market by companies from across the border. Supporters of free trade made strenuous efforts to direct their attention to the prospects for greater export, which in some cases could be expected to more than offset any domestic losses. They succeeded in convincing some of the businesses that had initially opposed the negotiations to come out in favor of the agreement.

Changing the Ratification Procedure

Bargainers can try to bypass their most troublesome constituency. Israeli prime minister Menachem Begin did this in 1978 when he held a national referendum to approve the peace accord he had negotiated at Camp David with Egypt's president Anwar el-Sadat. Peace talks with Egypt had provoked vocal criticism from his own party, Likud. If Begin had brought the accord to the Knesset for ratification—the normal procedure—he would have given his opponents a well-publicized opportunity to embarrass him, by forcing him to rely on the Labor Party for support. Begin justified a national referendum on the grounds that the agreement with Egypt was such a major decision that it required direct approval of the electorate.

This tactic can be used against any kind of constituency. However, it works only in those rare instances when bargainers have the power to change the rules. Ratification is more often an immutable process whose requirements are established by precedent or law.

Bypassing Ratification

Bargainers can sometimes outflank their opposition by dispensing altogether with ratification. Jimmy Carter did this with the SALT II agreement, which he was forced to withdraw from the Senate when it became apparent that it would go down to defeat. He treated SALT II as an executive agreement and announced his intention to abide by its terms. Arms control opponents were enraged, and presidential candidate Ronald Reagan promised to disavow the agreement if elected. Once in office, Reagan found it too costly politically to violate the precedent set by Carter's adherence to the agreement.

From Theory to Practice

Ratification follows agreement, but it is a mistake to defer consideration of ratification until after an agreement has been reached. Many, if not most of the tactics we have analyzed in this chapter need to be implemented during the bargaining stage. Co-option should be attempted before any bargaining begins. The choice of tactic may also influence the nature or details of the agreement that you seek. Bargaining and ratification are thus part and parcel of the same process and need to be considered in tandem.

The links between bargaining and ratification make it essential that you consider ratification at the very outset of the bargaining process. If you wait until agreement is reached, some tactics will no longer be open to you, or will be more difficult or costly to implement. An early start on ratification could make the difference between success and failure.

The step-by-step analysis that follows will help you frame the ratification problem and cue you when you need to make or implement choices.

1. *Will your agreement need to be ratified?* If not, you can proceed to the chapter on implementation. If ratification is essential, you need to familiarize yourself with the parameters of the process. Is there a constitutional, legal, or other requirement for ratification? Who needs to ratify the agreement? What is the ratification procedure? If it is by vote, by what majority? Do you have any choice or leeway with regard to any of these conditions?
2. *Do you expect any problems with ratification?* Sometimes, ratification can be taken for granted. The House of Lords will never reject legislation sent to it by the House of Commons, but it may suggest changes. Other bodies function as "rubber stamps." Presidents or trustees of universities usually have ultimate authority for approving new appointments or other arrangements negotiated by departments, deans, or provosts. However, they rarely if ever overrule the decisions of the operating officers of their university.

In dealing with rubber stamp bodies, it is usually acceptable to present them with *faits accomplis*. This keeps them at an arm's length and confronts them with agreements that everybody lower down supports. However, when consensus is lacking, or when the agreement has major, novel implications, it is probably wiser to keep them informed but uninvolved in the negotiations.

3. *What kind of constituency do you confront?* When ratification is not guaranteed, you may need to make a major investment of time and resources to achieve it. Your choice of tactics should be dictated by the nature of the ratification problem and the resources at your disposal. The first step in scoping out the problem should be to determine the character of the constituency you confront.

The identity of a constituency can sometimes be deceptive. It may appear to be an individual or group with formal authority over ratification but in practice be another individual or group who has influence over the formal authority. My wife recently mediated a divorce in which the final arbiter of any settlement turned out to be the wife's father. In the SALT II agreement, the Joint Chiefs of Staff were a dominant constituency, even though they had no constitutional role in the ratification process. You may need to look beyond the formal organizational chart to see who really exercises power and then direct your major efforts toward them. It is a waste of time to try to win over parties who are not essential or who cannot be influenced directly.

We have identified and analyzed three types of constituencies. In practice, you may confront more than one at a time. A dominant or blackmail constituency may have a right of veto over ratification, but to secure ratification you may need to appease other parties as well. Jimmy Carter satisfied the joint chiefs but not enough senators to ratify his arms control agreement. If you confront a complicated situation like this, you need to figure out the minimum number of individuals or groups you need to satisfy, isolate, or bypass, and the proper tactics for dealing with each of them.

Blackmail constituencies. These constituencies seek to exploit their power over ratification to gain concessions on unrelated issues. They need to be bypassed, isolated, or bought off. Bypassing or isolation are the preferred choices, but they may not be available to you. The feasibility of these tactics will depend on the nature of the ratification process the agreement would face and the resources available to you.

If a blackmail constituency cannot be bypassed or isolated, you will need to buy it off. These constituencies are rarely shy about making their demands known. If they can be satisfied at little cost, you should not hesitate to buy them off, unless you are concerned about setting a precedent. Buying them off may be preferable and cheaper than trying to bypass or isolate them. Problems arise when satisfying blackmail constituencies requires excessive resources or commitments. You can try bargaining down their price. Efforts to develop other alternatives (e.g., bypass and isolation) can strengthen your bargaining position vis-à-vis these constituencies.

The worst case arises when blackmail constituencies cannot be bypassed or isolated and ask too much to be bought off. In this circumstance, you need to reconsider whether negotiation is worth the cost. If the resulting agreement would be unratifiable or cost too much to ratify, you might be better off adopting another strategy for advancing your interests. As blackmail strategies will achieve nothing if there is no agreement to ratify, the threat not to negotiate, backed up perhaps by the exploration of alternatives, may convince the constituency to lower their demands.

Dominant constituencies. These constituencies also have the power to block ratification, but unlike blackmail constituencies, they have a direct, substantive interest in any agreement and its terms. To decide what tactic, or combination of tactics, is most effective in dealing with a dominant constituency, it is first necessary to learn more about its interests and the outcome it seeks. If those interests are compatible with yours, its preferences and yours may not be that far apart. It may be possible to co-opt the constituency or rely on other cooperative tactics that attempt to satisfy its interests and give it a stake in any agreement.

Dominant constituencies whose interests are more divergent from yours are more likely to oppose any agreement regardless of the efforts you make to address their needs or bring them into the bargaining. To the extent that their interests are incompatible with the agreement, you will need to isolate, bypass, divide, threaten, or make side payments to them to secure ratification.

Multiple constituencies. Ratification in the presence of multiple constituencies usually requires coalition building. To put together a successful coalition, you need to determine the minimum number of individuals or groups required to achieve the necessary majority, and figure out what it will take to win their support. If the cost is not excessive, you might consider building a slightly larger coalition, to protect against last minute defections, or threats of defection used to extract additional concessions. If one or more of the components of your coalition is too difficult or costly to win over, look into the possibility of substituting other individuals or groups. If you can build a larger coalition than you need, individual members will not be as essential, and you may not have to pay them as much for their support. In this circumstance, a larger coalition may actually cost you less to build.

There are several tactics that can be used to build coalitions. These include co-option, sequencing, side payments, divide and rule, and threats. Your choice of tactics will depend on the power and interests of the individuals or groups with whom you must bargain and on the extent of your own resources and leverage. In dealing with multiple constituencies, it may be necessary to weaken opposing factions by threatening or isolating them. This may reduce their ability to build an opposing majority coalition.

4. *Should you reconsider your bargaining goals?* To gain the support of dominant or multiple constituencies you generally need to reward them in some manner. To do this, you may have to alter your bargaining goals to take their preferences into account. The more advance notice you have about what it will take to satisfy critical constituencies, the better off you will be. It is sometimes necessary to think about ratification and its requirements even before establishing your own bargaining goals. This will help you to decide whether bargaining is feasible before you have invested a lot of time and resources in it. If bargaining is feasible, and you have a reasonable idea of what an agreement will take to ratify, you can then decide whether you would be better off bargaining or pursuing some other, nonbargaining alternative.

Chapter 11

Implementation

Some agreements are simple to execute. Tailpipe Harry hands over the keys and documents to the car in return for your certified check. Other agreements require more elaborate implementation. Divorce agreements typically stipulate a distribution of assets, monthly child support payments over a period of years, and visitation rights for the spouse without custody. Agreements of this kind are meaningless if not successfully implementable. Bargainers accordingly need to pay as much attention to implementation as they do to negotiation and ratification.

Implementation cannot be taken for granted. Students of family law report that more than half of all divorce agreements involving alimony or child support payments are not honored after three years. The civil court dockets are filled with cases of businesses suing other businesses for noncompliance with contracts. Cease-fire agreements and peace treaties are equally precarious. As this book goes to press, the Khmer Rouge in Cambodia, UNITA in Angola, and Serbian "irregulars" in Bosnia are using violence to block the implementation of accords to which they are signatories.

Motives for Noncompliance

Bargainers will try to impede the implementation of agreements they feel coerced into signing. This is one reason why divorce settlements have such a bad record of compliance. Bargainers who are satisfied with an agreement at the time it was made can subsequently balk at implementation if their interests change. The classic case is the guilt-ridden husband who initiates a divorce and agrees to pay his wife a lot of money but subsequently meets another woman and begins to feel "ripped off" by his divorce settlement. In business, companies negotiate contracts to sell goods or services at an agreed-upon price. If the market value of what they sell rises steeply between the signing of the contract and the date of delivery, they may be reluctant to consummate the deal, because they could now charge higher prices to other customers.

A colleague of mine at a midwestern university was a victim of market-driven noncompliance. He directs an institute whose new building was to be ready for occupancy at the beginning of the 1993 academic year. The construction contracts were let at the height of the recession, when companies were desperate for business. But the local economy later picked up, and construction increased considerably, making it possible for contractors to demand significantly better terms. Several of the subcontractors on the university's building deserted that project to work at more lucrative jobs. The building was not ready on time, but the institute was expected to move on schedule from its old quarters.

A third generic cause of implementation problems is incomplete or ambiguous agreements. Bargainers sometimes reach agreements in principle but fail to discuss or agree on what is required to put them into effect. Subsequent efforts at implementation bring to light different and incompatible interpretations of the agreement.

At Camp David in 1978, President Anwar el-Sadat and Prime Minister Menachem Begin reached their breakthrough agreement: Israel would return the Sinai Peninsula to Egypt who in turn would recognize the state of Israel and its right to have secure borders. Both leaders went home convinced that they had transformed the politics of the Middle East. Subsequent discussions between their staffs revealed serious disagreements about what territory constituted the Sinai, the pace of Israel's withdrawal, and the nature and timing of the normalization of relations between the two countries.

Similar problems plagued attempts by the former communist countries of Eastern Europe to establish joint business ventures with Western companies. Even agreements that were painstakingly negotiated ran into serious difficulties in practice because of the different expectations of the two sides. In the Czech Republic, large industrial plants provide hot water and electricity to local communities. Czech officials who sold the plants to foreigners expected the free supply of utilities to continue, but at some plants, the new Western managers, who knew nothing about this practice before they arrived on the scene, insisted that the communities pay for their utilities. Disagreements also arose over terms of payment, choice of subcontractors, and treatment of labor.

It is hardly surprising that capitalist investors from the West and former socialist officials from the East had different conceptions of how to do business or that these differences became apparent only in the nitty-gritty of implementation. But such problems also arise between parties who share the same culture. An acquaintance of mine reached a relatively amicable divorce agreement with his former wife only to have it break down less than a week later. The problem was visitation rights. His six-year-old daughter is supposed to spend every other weekend with him, but his wife, who lives in another city, refuses to transport her to and from the train station. She insists that it is her ex-husband's responsibility to arrange for door-to-door transportation.

Vulnerable Agreements

Certain kinds of agreements are easier to violate than others. The most vulnerable are those that require sustained action by the other side. Implementation of a used car sale may entail nothing more than exchange of a certified check in return for the car, keys, title, and registration; but a divorce settlement may stipulate the sale of property and subsequent distribution of the proceeds, monthly child support payments for many years, and visitation rights that require cooperation by now hostile parents. Many commercial agreements require more cooperation during implementation than they did during bargaining.

Agreements that involve third parties are more difficult to implement. Labor-management agreements often need to be sold to union members or company boards. Either group may be unhappy with the settlement yet feel constrained to approve it. If they are very much opposed to aspects of the agreement, they may try subsequently to sabotage its implementation. Labor unions may "work to rule," to force renegotiation of the contract. Companies may refuse to follow environmental guidelines or antidumping rules negotiated by their government. Quasi-independent military forces may refuse to honor cease-fires negotiated by their political representatives, as has happened in Angola, Cambodia, Yugoslavia, and Rwanda.

Agreements that require a lot of resources to implement are more likely to run into trouble. Companies may borrow a lot of money to expand production, in the expectation that the increased production will generate more than enough profits to repay the debt and the interest on it. But a severe contraction in the market might result in decreased profits and make repayment difficult. This problem befell many Third World countries who borrowed money in the expansionist 1980s and a decade later were unable to service their debts, let alone repay the principal.

Another common cause of implementation problems is unclear or ambiguous agreements. They provide loopholes that one or both sides can try to exploit. On occasion, one or even both sides may deliberately want to leave some ambiguity in the agreement, to leave a way out should their interests change. More often than not, though, ambiguity is unintentional. Under pressure to reach an agreement, both sides may overlook issues that subsequently turn out to be critical. During the 1973 Middle East War, Henry Kissinger flew to Moscow to negotiate an Egyptian-Israeli cease-fire with Soviet premier Leonid Brezhnev. The two men and their aides worked through the night to hammer out an agreement. Only later, when the cease-fire proved difficult to enforce, did they realize they had not discussed or agreed upon any procedures for implementation and verification.

Implementation problems are more likely to arise when the cost of noncompliance is low. This is another reason why divorce settlements are so frequently violated. It is comparatively easy to evade alimony and child support payments. Women—who are usually the recipients of these payments—are often the victims of a "catch-22." In order to press their claim to these payments, they must hire lawyers, who do not come cheap, and must accordingly wait until their ex-husbands are far enough in arrears to make filing a claim worthwhile. They may then encounter judges who decide that they do not need the payments, because they have lived without them for such a long interval.

Similar problems plague other kinds of agreements. The low costs of noncompliance seem to have played a determining role in the Nestlé company's response to the criticism of its sales of infant formula in Africa. Formula feeding is medically disastrous in much of Africa because mothers mix the formula with contaminated water that gives diarrhea to their children. Under international pressure, Nestlé agreed to halt its advertising campaign against breast feeding and stop dumping formula on the African market. The company nevertheless continued to sell millions of dollars worth of formula throughout Africa. Its executives have been accused of signing an agreement they had no intention of honoring, for the good publicity that agreement was expected to bring.

Improving Compliance

The best way to ensure compliance is to negotiate an agreement that the other side is equally committed to making work. When a signatory is convinced that an agreement is in its interest, it is more likely to abide by the terms and assist in carrying them out. Dissatisfaction with the terms and anger at the process combine to provide strong incentives to violate the agreement at the first opportunity.

The sad history of divorce settlements reveals an elemental truth about bargaining: tough bargains can sometimes be counterproductive. If the other side feels "ripped off," it is likely to look for some way out of the agreement or some way to "get even." When implementation requires the active and continued cooperation of the other side, antagonizing that party courts disaster.

There is much to be said for not extracting the last pound of flesh, and even for allowing the other side to emerge with more than it expected. In the Cuban missile crisis, President Kennedy reaped a handsome dividend from restraint. Khrushchev, we now know, was prepared to remove the Soviet missiles from Cuba to prevent an American invasion of that island. Kennedy had no intention of attacking Cuba unless it became necessary in order to get the missiles out. Kennedy was also prepared to promise not to invade Cuba if that would make it easier for Khrushchev to withdraw the missiles. Khrushchev was surprised and impressed by Kennedy's restraint, especially by his decision not to exploit the discovery of Soviet missiles in Cuba as a pretext to overthrow the Castro regime. Khrushchev came away from the crisis convinced that Kennedy was as committed to avoiding war as he was. The new respect each leader had for the other provided the basis and incentive for their subsequent moves towards arms control and détente.

Another strategy for securing compliance is renegotiation. This should be considered when postnegotiation developments have led the other side to conclude that the agreement is no longer in their interests. In 1969, Newfoundland signed a contract to sell Quebec electric power generated from Churchill Falls in Labrador. Newfoundland agreed to provide 5.2 million kilowatts a year for forty years at a price of under three mills per kilowatt-hour. Quebec has the option to renew for twenty-five years at two mills per kilowatt-hour. With the dramatic rise of energy costs during the 1980s, Quebec has reaped huge profits from the resale of Newfoundland power.

The contract became a cause of severe friction between the two Canadian provinces. Quebec has categorically refused to renegotiate the agreement, and Newfoundland sought to get even by diverting some of the water that flows over Churchill Falls. In 1984, Canada's Supreme Court ruled this diversion illegal. In the late 1980s, Newfoundland's premier, Clyde Wells, became one of the leading opponents of the Meech Lake Agreement, which would have given special constitutional rights to Quebec. Political analysts believe that Wells' opposition was motivated by his province's anger at Quebec. The American decision to renegotiate the debts of Brazil and Mexico represents a more positive response to changed circumstances. As we have observed, it succeeded in forestalling defaults that would have been costly to all parties concerned.

Renegotiation is a variant of the strategy of reward. Strategies of punishment can also be used to improve the probability of compliance. Many agreements have clauses that establish penalties for noncompliance or dilatory compliance. Business contracts routinely include delivery schedules with fines for late delivery. If those fines are sufficiently great and readily enforceable, the obligated party will have a strong incentive to honor the agreement.

Some agreements go a step further and set up procedures for determining whether or not the signatories are in compliance with the agreement. The SALT II agreement had as many clauses about verification and adjudication of disputes about compliance as it had clauses stipulating substantive arms control measures. In the course of the 1980s, each side charged the other with violations and invoked clauses of the agreement to substantiate its claims.

Vagueness versus Precision

Up to now, we have stressed the dangers of imprecise or incomplete agreements. They may mask important disagreements, make implementation more difficult, and permit loopholes that allow the other side to walk away from the agreement at little or no cost. But in some situations ambiguity can confer bargaining advantages, and it is important to know how they can be exploited.

Imprecise or incomplete agreements can serve as insurance policies. In an uncertain environment where interests or costs are unpredictable, one may want an escape clause from any agreement. Conversely, when agreement is expected to be advantageous, it is usually advisable to make it difficult for the other side to back out.

It sometimes pays to reach an agreement in principle and to address the details of the agreement and its implementation at a later stage. This can be a productive approach when the other side wants an agreement but is likely to resist the compromises or concessions necessary for its implementation. An agreement in principle can significantly reshape its cost calculus and make those concessions more palatable. If the agreement elicits a favorable response from important constituencies the cost of a subsequent breakdown in negotiations will be raised. The process of negotiation can also encourage among the participants a commitment to reaching an agreement; they may have spent long hours preparing for and participating in negotiations and understandably would like to see some positive outcome to their efforts. Either phenomenon can be exploited in an attempt to push the other side into making compromises or accepting terms it would have rejected in the absence of an agreement in principle.

In 1991, IBM and Apple Computer reached an agreement to create Taligent, a joint venture to develop hardware and software. At the time, IBM and Apple were rapidly losing their respective shares of the personal computer market. Executives of both companies hoped that cooperation would boost confidence among investors and lead to products that would give them a competitive edge. Apple and IBM represent two very different corporate cultures. Not surprisingly, their first concrete effort at collaboration—PowerPC, a processing unit that both companies intend to use in their machines—encountered all kinds of organizational difficulties. Both companies persevered and made the kinds of accommodations that were necessary, in part because they expected that the costs of failing at their well-publicized commitment to cooperate would be extraordinarily high.

The Cuban missile crisis provides another example of the benefits of an agreement in principle. The crisis ended on Sunday 28 October, when Khrushchev agreed to withdraw the Soviet missiles in Cuba in return for a public pledge from Kennedy not to invade Cuba and a private promise from him to remove American Jupiter missiles from Turkey. Nothing was put in writing about implementation beyond the stipulation that the Cuban missile withdrawal would be carried out under the supervision of the United Nations. It took several months of intensive and sometimes tense negotiations between representatives of the two superpowers to flesh out the details of the agreement. The Americans insisted that the Soviets also withdraw their IL-28 bombers from Cuba, while the Soviets maintained that this was not part of the deal. The Soviets also ran into trouble with Fidel Castro, who opposed the withdrawal and early on tried to block its implementation by surrounding a Soviet missile base with Cuban troops.

Throughout the period of the postcrisis negotiations, the United States kept its military forces at a high stage of readiness and its ships at sea ready to establish a more restrictive blockade of Cuba. The Soviet Union, by contrast, had lost most of its leverage when it announced its willingness in principle to withdraw its missiles. The Kennedy administration exploited this bargaining advantage to push Moscow to accept its conditions on several critical issues, including the withdrawal of the IL-28s. In retrospect, we see that Kennedy did the right thing by separating principle and detail; it eased the achievement of his objectives in both areas.

These several examples drive home the need to consider early in any negotiation how complete and precise an agreement to seek. To make an intelligent decision you must consider your own and the other side's commitment to an agreement, the relative difficulty of securing an agreement in detail versus one in principle, and the likelihood that an agreement in principle can be exploited to gain concessions from the other side concerning the substance of the agreement or its implementation. These decisions can be difficult to make in the absence of good information about the other side's framing of the bargaining encounter. Bargainers need to use the techniques described earlier for eliciting information about the other side's preferences.

From Theory to Practice

Like ratification, implementation should be considered beforehand by bargainers. Implementation requirements should inform your choice of goals and bargaining strategies. By thinking about implementation before bargaining, you may be able to structure an agreement that makes implementation easier and cooperation by the other side more probable. Your answers to the following questions should guide your approach to implementation.

1. *Is your agreement self-executing?* If so, you do not need to plot an approach to implementation. However, if execution of your agreement is likely to require the cooperation of the other side, you need to work through the remaining questions.

2. *In what ways does your agreement require cooperation?* When you have identified the ways in which implementation requires actions by the other side (or third parties), ask yourself if there is anything that can be done to reduce this dependence. This is the first and by far the preferable approach to implementation.

    When dependence on the cooperation of the other side cannot be avoided, you can try as far as possible to make that cooperation self-executing. One possibility in this regard is to require the other side to carry out all or most of its commitments at the time the agreement is signed. This makes subsequent defection difficult or impossible. A variant that is sometimes possible when money or other tangible assets are involved is to require the other side to set up an escrow account or hand the assets over to an executor who can subsequently distribute them in accordance with the terms of the agreement.

3. *What motives might the other side have to defect?* The second approach to implementation tries to reduce the other side's incentives to get out of the agreement. Earlier in the chapter we identified four possible reasons for defection: feeling "ripped off," changed interests, inadequate resources, and the low cost of defection. Two other conditions, incomplete or ambiguous agreements, while not motives themselves, provide opportunities to those wanting to defect for other reasons.

    Are any of these reasons or conditions present in your bargaining situation or agreement? If not, be careful not to create them. Probably the most important rule in this regard is to avoid compelling the other side to settle for an agreement that it does not see as in its interests. As we noted earlier, the strategy of punishment can lead to Pyrrhic victories in the form of unenforceable agreements.

4. *Which implementation strategy is most appropriate?* We identified four strategies useful in improving the chances of successful implementation of agreements. These strategies address different motives for defection:

Saving face. This is most effective with a bargainer who feels that it is being coerced into an agreement. It is important to give the other side something that will make it value the agreement. How much you need to concede depends on the other side's interests and how dependent you are on it for implementation. If the other side feels coerced, it is likely to show its resentment. Be wary of feigned resentment that may be an attempt to gain extra concessions.

Renegotiation. This is a postagreement strategy for dealing with problems that develop or only become apparent in the course of implementation. Renegotiation is a useful way of dealing with changed interests, inadequate resources, and incomplete or ambiguous agreements.

Agreement in detail. When implementation is critical and the negotiators are not constrained from discussing implementation, it is probably wise to incorporate the terms of implementation in the agreement. You should identify what kinds of resources, commitments, or cooperation will be required and compel the other side to agree to do what is necessary as part of the overall agreement. At the very least, this kind of attention to detail makes it more difficult for the other side to engage in postagreement blackmail. That is, to refuse to carry out critical steps of implementation unless you make additional concessions.

Penalties. A step beyond agreement in detail is the stipulation of penalties for noncompliance with the agreement. Enforceable penalty clauses can significantly raise the cost of defection. The key to their success is enforceability. If you can get the other side to commit itself in writing to implementation procedures, and you have a forum, like a court of law, where you can appeal for redress or enforcement or both, penalties will give teeth to the agreement. Where it is feasible, you can insist on prepayment of a penalty, to be held in escrow and returned upon successful implementation of the agreement. Landlords do this routinely when they demand a security deposit.

If no enforceable penalties have been written into the agreement, you will have to rely on renegotiation to elicit cooperation or the strategy of punishment to compel it.

Part 4 Problem Shooting

Chapter 12

Misperceptions and Misjudgments

The strategies of punishment and reward try to gain the other side's assent to outcomes they would otherwise reject by changing their estimates of the value of those outcomes. The strategy of rewards does this by making outcomes more attractive, the strategy of punishment by making their rejection less attractive.

Both strategies assume that it is possible to understand and change other parties' preferences, but in the real world, preferences and signals are rarely transparent. Bargainers most often need to estimate others' preferences on the basis of incomplete information. If they guess incorrectly, their rewards or threats may be inappropriate or insufficient. When they guess correctly, their signals of rewards or threats must be understood by the other side. If the parties use different contexts to frame and interpret signals, misunderstandings are likely to arise. Poorly understood preferences or faulty communication can confound the strategies of rewards and punishments and undermine the search for accommodation.

Context

We have examined a number of key bargaining asymmetries, including resources, alternatives, interests, time, precedent, and reputation. These asymmetries confer bargaining advantages only when the two sides share the same understanding of them. If both agree that one of them has no alternative but to make a deal and is sorely pressed for time, the other can reasonably expect to drive a stiffer bargain. But if the bargainer who faces these constraints is able to hide them from the other side, it may conceivably avoid any ill consequences. A more serious problem arises when bargainers have different understandings of the same asymmetries. Suppose each side believes that it has more resources, more at stake, and is less constrained by time. The bargainers will have diametrically opposed estimates of the balance of power between them, and each side is likely to insist on terms that the other will reject as unreasonable.

In 1947, the Soviet Union rejected the Truman administration's offer of Marshall Plan aid. The administration regarded its offer of credits to the war-ravaged Soviet Union as an act of generosity. Stalin and his advisors viewed it as an act of desperation. As good Marxists, they reasoned that the United States was almost certain to suffer a postwar depression unless it could find adequate markets to absorb its industrial and agricultural surplus. If the Marshall Plan was a calculated attempt by the Truman administration to stave off economic chaos, they did not see why they should take American credits without receiving some kind of quid pro quo. The Soviet demand for concessions in return for accepting Marshall Plan aid infuriated the Americans, who interpreted it as gratuitously hostile behavior.

Similar misunderstandings confound interpersonal bargaining. In many American states, ex-wives are entitled to "PHT (putting hubby through)" compensation for financial contributions they have made to their husbands' education. The amount they receive is usually calculated on the basis of how much they have provided or how much their former spouse is expected to earn. There is often considerable disagreement, especially about the latter. Not long ago, my wife made an unsuccessful attempt to mediate a divorce settlement between a copy editor and a gynecologist. Both parties agreed that the wife, the copy editor, had supported the couple while the husband was in medical school and that about half his education had been paid for by her earnings and savings. She demanded a $500,000 settlement based on her contribution and the expectation that her former husband, who had recently entered a practice, would soon pull in big bucks. The husband was much less optimistic about his earning capacity and cited the rising costs of malpractice insurance and paperwork, government-imposed limitations on what he could charge for given procedures, and overcrowding in his specialty. He offered a $200,000 settlement, insisting that any more would drive him out of practice. Discussions that drew on diverse estimates of earning capacity made by independent professionals failed to resolve the controversy and the case went to court.

Many bargaining encounters fail because the parties involved have clashing estimates of the asymmetries involved. As in the case of Marshall Plan aid, they are unaware of their different readings of the context. But awareness of the problem does not necessarily facilitate resolution. As in the divorce mediation, the two sides can remain committed to their interpretations.

Different interpretations of context are not only the result of different interpretations of asymmetries. Bargainers may also be using entirely different frames of reference to conceptualize their encounter. When this happens, they are likely to talk past one other and base their promises of rewards or threats of punishment on false premises.

All these problems are well illustrated by the fifty-one-day siege of the Branch Davidian sect in Waco, Texas, in 1993. Experts subsequently called in to evaluate the performance of law enforcement agencies contended that bloodshed might have been averted if the FBI had used an appropriate frame of reference. FBI agents should have realized that they were dealing with a violent sect, many of whose members were prepared to die for their beliefs. Instead, they treated the confrontation as a hostage situation. They relied on basic principles of hostage negotiation and ignored or minimized evidence that indicated that this approach would not work. They were blind to the reality that sect members were there by choice and adhered to an ideology that glorified armed confrontation.

Because they framed Waco as a hostage situation, the agents did not consult with any authorities on cults. Several of these authorities, psychologists who regularly consult for the FBI and the Justice Department, insist that they would have advised against the use of threats and the prominent display of governmental firepower. In their view, this only solidified David Koresh's hold over sect members, by confirming his prophecy that evil forces were arrayed against them and that salvation would come in the form of violent death. If these authorities are correct, the FBI's strategy helped to provoke the outcome it sought to avoid.

Preferences

To succeed in making a particular outcome more palatable to another party, threats of punishment and promises of rewards must shift that party's preferences by the desired amount *and* in the desired direction. Threats or promises based on a faulty understanding of another's preferences can have the unintended effect of strengthening those preferences and making agreement less rather than more likely.

Some years back, I was provided a vivid demonstration of this phenomenon by my then five-year-old son, Eli. He had hit his two-year-old brother, David, several times during the course of the day. The reason for Eli's hostility was transparent: David had been ill with the flu and had received a lot of attention from his parents. I told Eli that if he hit his brother again I would take away his LEGO tiles (there was nothing Eli valued as much at the time as his LEGO collection).

Five minutes later Eli hit his brother in full sight of his parents. I took away his LEGO. In my office the next day I thought about the incident and wondered if my threat had not encouraged Eli to hit his brother. Eli was hostile toward David but may also have felt guilt about his hostility. If so, he was cross-pressured until I resolved his dilemma by my threat. With the threat in place, Eli could express his hostility toward his brother and then expiate his guilt through punishment. Perhaps this is why Eli accepted the loss of his LEGO tiles quite calmly.

There are many corporate and international analogues to this familial deterrence failure. They are analogous in the sense that the threats involved provoked the behavior they were designed to deter. They differ, of course, in that the calculations of interest were conscious and economic or political, not unconscious and psychological. The origins of the Spanish-American War of 1898–99 provide an interesting example.

An insurrection in Cuba which Spanish forces could not suppress put Spain on a collision course with the United States. American investments in Cuba were endangered, and a yellow fever epidemic, caused by deteriorating sanitary conditions on the island, was spreading to the southeastern part of the United States. Congressional insistence that Spain get out of Cuba led President Cleveland and subsequently President McKinley to explore a variety of diplomatic solutions. None of them proved acceptable to successive Spanish governments, who feared a military revolt if they made any concessions to the rebels. McKinley's demands on Spain in the aftermath of the destruction of the *Maine* in Havana Harbor inflamed Spanish opinion, further restricting the government's freedom of action. The president and Congress nevertheless expected that continued pressure would bring Madrid to its senses. Instead, it provoked war.

Spanish leaders were pulled in opposite directions by public opinion and the army. The war in Cuba was increasingly unpopular at home; continued prosecution of the conflict raised the risk of insurrection and civil war. But the Spanish military would not countenance negotiations with the rebels. American threats of intervention appeared to offer Spanish leaders a way out of their dilemma. If Washington declared war, they reasoned, the Americans were likely to invade Cuba and compel Spain to renounce sovereignty over the island. Public opinion would be satisfied. So would the army, which would have defended its honor against an acceptable adversary. By presenting Spain with an ultimatum, McKinley unwittingly played into Spanish hands.

Rewards can be as counterproductive as threats when they strengthen existing preferences rather than shift them. Britain and France appeased Hitler in the 1930s in the expectation of preventing another European war. Their appeasement was based on the assumption that Hitler had limited territorial objectives that could be satisfied by concessions. But Hitler was insatiable, and appeasement encouraged him to raise new demands by convincing him that the Western powers lacked the will to go to war in defense of the territorial status quo.

American policy toward Saddam Hussein illustrates the failure of both rewards and punishments. During the two years prior to Iraq's invasion of Kuwait, President George Bush wrote several letters to Saddam assuring him of America's goodwill. The administration continued to give Iraq credits with which to buy wheat and barley, even though the Department of Agriculture recommended that they be stopped because they were consistently being diverted to the purchase of military equipment. The reward of aid did nothing to moderate Saddam, and may have encouraged him to believe that the United States would do nothing more than protest verbally his invasion of Kuwait.

Following the Iraqi occupation of Kuwait, Bush gave Saddam a deadline for withdrawal from Kuwait and, together with America's European and Middle Eastern allies, carried out a major military buildup in the region, to be in a position to liberate Kuwait by force if necessary. Bush and some of his principal advisors expected compellence to work; the United States and its allies had overwhelming military power and were demonstrably prepared to use it to achieve their political goals.

The allied buildup undeniably made the continued occupation of Kuwait more costly, but it also made retreat more costly. By his inflammatory rhetoric, George Bush transformed Kuwait into a personal confrontation. If Saddam backed down, he would suffer a public humiliation. His dream of dominating the Arab world would come to an abrupt end, and he might suffer such a loss of legitimacy at home that it would prove difficult to hold on to power. By going to war, he could save face and, like Nasser in 1956 and 1967, might snatch political victory from the jaws of military defeat. The Arab masses could be expected to rally to his support—especially if Israel was drawn into the fight—and compel a change in the policy of those moderate Arab states arrayed against him. In Saddam's calculus, resistance to superior military force, even though it meant losing the war, looked like the better bet.

These examples illustrate two different ways in which strategies of punishment and rewards can fail. For the Spanish government and Hitler they reduced (or appeared to reduce) the costs of pursuing their preferred policies and made them correspondingly more attractive. For Saddam Hussein, George Bush's attempt at compellence made the costs of backing down appear prohibitive.

Both kinds of failure have the same underlying cause: a fundamentally flawed appreciation of the other side's preferences. With Hitler, the misunderstood element was motive. Chamberlain and his associates mistakenly believed that Hitler had limited territorial objectives. In the Cuban crisis, Spanish preferences were shaped by domestic constraints that American leaders knew nothing about. President McKinley could not imagine that his threat of war would be welcomed by Spanish leaders as a possible way out of their political dilemma. George Bush similarly failed to understand the foreign and domestic pressures that drove Saddam to attack Kuwait and subsequently kept him from retreating before the American military buildup and ultimatum.

These policy failures might have been prevented by more accurate information about the motives of the other actors and the constraints acting on them. Much of this information was unavailable, as is often the case in bargaining situations. Bargainers are sometimes unaware of their own motives. When they think them through, they may try to mask or mislead others about them. Knowledge about constraints can be equally difficult to come by. It often requires inside information about the workings of another company, organization, or political system. This too is difficult to obtain when the other side attempts to keep the information under wraps.

Better information does not necessarily lead to better estimates of motives or preferences. By 1938, Hitler had provided unambiguous evidence of his aggressive intentions. Saddam Hussein had done likewise prior to Iraq's invasion of Kuwait. The appeasers in both situations were strongly motivated to believe that a strategy of rewards would elicit cooperation. The British and French people looked on the prospect of another war with revulsion. Because resistance to Hitler was politically unpopular, many British and French leaders convinced themselves that the only available alternative, appeasement, would succeed despite the evidence to the contrary.

The Bush administration's failure in Iraq may have been the result of a similar dynamic. The United States had drawn close to Iraq because both countries had conflicts with Iran. American officials wanted to believe that Saddam could be won over by rewards because they were keen to use Iraq as a counterweight to Iran. Like Neville Chamberlain, George Bush and Secretary of State James Baker chose to ignore or explain away all the evidence indicating that Saddam was a tyrant ready to go to war to dominate the region.

The Double Whammy

Estimates of preferences can also be confounded by the miscalculations of those whose preferences are being estimated. Faced with the prospect of the Spanish-American War, Spanish leaders saw war as attractive, because they expected a brief and limited conflict that would free them of the burden of Cuba. They failed to consider that war would also prompt American invasions of Puerto Rico and the Philippines, the destruction of the Spanish fleet in Manila Bay, and revolution at home.

In the Persian Gulf crisis, both the United States and Iraq formulated their preferences on the basis of major miscalculations. Saddam's preference for war over retreat was the result of his gross underestimation of the costs of war and an equal exaggeration of its expected benefits. George Bush believed that Saddam would withdraw from Kuwait when confronted with a massive allied military buildup in Saudi Arabia, because he mistakenly believed that war would result in Saddam's overthrow.

Miscalculations of this kind are inevitable in the complex environments where bargaining often takes place. Saddam was mistaken but not unreasonable in his expectation that an American attack would cause throughout the Middle East a groundswell of sympathy among Arab masses and the replacement of moderate regimes by radicals sympathetic to Iraq's cause. This erroneous prediction was also made by many Middle East experts in the West on the eve of the war. Other miscalculations are less excusable. Cases in point include Saddam's apparent belief that he would have several days after the expiry of the American ultimatum to reach a political settlement and that the Republican Guards could offer credible resistance to allied forces.

The common propensity to misjudge the context of others' preferences constitutes a serious impediment to successful bargaining. Understanding the other side's preferences requires knowing something about its goals and constraints but also about the ways in which it might misconstrue the bargaining environment and your preferences. Such insight is rare, which makes estimating preferences very difficult and renders the strategies of rewards and punishment uncertain, if necessary, tools.

Signals

Threats of punishment and promises of rewards need to be communicated effectively to their targets. This is sometimes a relatively straightforward process. Two individuals who know each other well may be able to exchange the most nuanced messages. But communication can be very difficult between strangers or people with tense or hostile relations. Communication is also difficult across organizational and national cultures.

There are three generic kinds of communication problems in bargaining: signals are dismissed as noise, noise is mistaken for signals, and signals are recognized for what they are but misinterpreted. Any of these problems can prove fatal to the negotiation process.

The Falklands/Malvinas conflict illustrates the first of these problems: signals that are dismissed as noise. On 2 April 1982, Argentine Marines stormed ashore at Port Stanley, the capital of the British dependency of the Falkland Islands. Prior to the invasion, the Argentine junta dropped many hints about its intentions. In late March, the Argentine fleet put to sea in the full glare of publicity: military leaves were canceled, and the Argentine news agency reported that the marine regiment aboard the flotilla had been issued food, arms, and ammunition. Four days before the invasion, Uruguay, at Argentina's request, asked the British government if it wanted Falklands' residents airlifted to safety "before the invasion." These signals were intended to convey Argentina's desperation and willingness to use force and to convince Britain to open serious negotiations. The Thatcher government missed many of the signals and dismissed others as bluff. The junta was then compelled by the momentum of events to carry out the invasion.

In the Cuban missile crisis, noise was repeatedly mistaken for signals.

On Wednesday 25 October, the *Washington Post* carried a column by the prominent journalist Walter Lippmann that called for the United States to dismantle its Jupiter missiles in Turkey as a quid pro quo for withdrawal of the Soviet missiles in Cuba. The Soviet embassy in Washington incorrectly read the column as a feeler put out by the White House and so advised Moscow. On Friday afternoon, Khrushchev wrote to Kennedy expressing willingness to remove the missiles in Cuba in return for a noninvasion pledge. On Saturday morning, apprised of the Lippmann column, Khrushchev sent another cable to Kennedy demanding the removal of the Jupiter missiles in addition to the noninvasion pledge. The president and his advisors could not understand why Khrushchev had suddenly decided to up the ante; they speculated that hardliners in the Kremlin had forced him to pursue a tougher line.

Moscow's estimates of American intentions were also shaped by noise. On Saturday morning, an American U-2 on an air sampling mission that was to have been canceled mistakenly wandered into Soviet airspace over the Kamchatka Peninsula. Soviet generals advised Khrushchev that the flight was deliberate and possibly a last-minute intelligence mission before launching a nuclear attack against the Soviet Union. On Sunday, the KGB (the Committee for State Security) office in Washington sent a high-priority message to Moscow reporting that Kennedy was going to make another television address that evening. Khrushchev and his advisors worried that the president was going to announce an invasion of Cuba, or possibly an attack on the Soviet Union. The KGB was misinformed; one of the American networks had advertised a rebroadcast of Kennedy's earlier address announcing the naval quarantine of Cuba. That afternoon, the KGB, which had been tailing Kennedy since the crisis began, correctly reported that the president had just left for church. Khrushchev and his colleagues pondered the significance of the report. Some of them speculated that the president had gone to church to pray before giving the order to destroy the Soviet Union.

The fog of crisis was just as thick in Washington. On Saturday morning, Khrushchev's confusing cable arrived. This was followed by a report from the navy that a Soviet ship was preparing to challenge the blockade line. Then the White House learned that Soviet forces in Cuba had shot down an American reconnaissance aircraft with a surface-to-air missile. The last two developments were noise; neither was a signal from the Kremlin. Khrushchev knew nothing about the ship, which in any case halted before reaching the blockade line, or about the U-2 that was shot down in violation of his orders not to fire at any American ships or planes unless Cuba was attacked. For the president and his advisors, all three events indicated Khrushchev's willingness, perhaps even intention, to challenge the United States militarily.

In the Falklands conflict and the Cuban missile crisis, signals were seriously misinterpreted. The British explained away the Argentine preparations for invasion as demonstrations of *machismo* intended to impress the Argentine public. The Thatcher government issued no public warning and sent no warships into the South Atlantic, for fear that demonstrations of resolve would only strengthen the hand of extremists in the Argentine junta. British passivity was interpreted in Buenos Aires as lack of resolve. Foreign Minister Nicanor Costa Méndes and his colleagues speculated that it was a signal from the politically constrained British to Argentina to invade and free them once and for all of the burden of the islands!

These communication problems derived from the same fundamental cause: leaders used different contexts to frame and interpret signals. When those contexts were contradictory or inappropriate, they encouraged false inferences.

Argentina and Britain approached the Falklands/Malvinas dispute from very different perspectives. For Argentina, the Islas Malvinas were national territory that had been occupied by a colonial power since 1833. British sovereignty over the islands was an atavism in a world that had witnessed numerous wars of liberation, bringing the era of colonialism to an end. Viewed in this light, it seemed far-fetched that the Thatcher government would try to reimpose its rule by force on a "liberated colony." World opinion and the constellation of international political forces militated against it. The analogy that sprang into Argentine minds was Goa, the Portuguese colonial enclave India had overrun without resistance in 1962. An early invasion scenario concocted by the Argentine navy was called Plan Goa.

The British politicians, press, and public felt a sense of obligation to the Falkland Islanders, who were of British stock and anxious to remain subjects of the Crown. The British regarded Argentina's threats of invasion as naked aggression on the part of a brutal dictatorship against a democratic and peace-loving people. For them, the relevant historical analogy was Hitler and the origins of World War II; British newspapers made frequent references to the events and lessons of that period. Chief among these was the need to stand up to aggression, because appeasement would whet the appetites of would-be aggressors everywhere. This consideration was decisive for the Thatcher government, which justified its need to retake the Falklands with the twin arguments that "aggression must not be allowed to succeed" and that "freedom must be protected against dictatorship."

If it was inconceivable to Argentina's junta that Britain would go to war to regain the Falklands, it was equally unthinkable to the Thatcher government that it would not do so if war proved the only way to compel Argentina to withdraw. The different historical contexts used by the two sets of national leaders to frame their dispute led not only to contrasting visions of justice but to quite different imperatives for action. Unfortunately, leaders and intelligence experts in London and Buenos Aires, while not altogether ignorant of the other's conceptualization of the problem, were unable to grasp the implications of that conceptualization for that country's behavior.

In the case of the Cuban missile crisis, the problem was the stereotyped understanding each side had of the other's political system. Soviet officials in Washington could not bring themselves to accept the implications of a free press. Knowing how journalism worked in their country, they were convinced that a politically sensitive column by a prominent journalist in the midst of an acute crisis must have been cleared, if not inspired, by the White House.

Back in Moscow, Khrushchev and his colleagues used Marxist-Leninist concepts to analyze the workings of the American government. They regarded the president and other officials as agents of capitalism and greatly underestimated their autonomy from Wall Street. The capitalist class was implacably hostile to Castro, because of the threat he posed to American hegemony in Latin America; their most influential organs of opinion, like *Time* magazine and the *Wall Street Journal,* repeatedly called for his overthrow. Khrushchev doubted that Kennedy could prevent the CIA and the military from using the opportunity provided by the crisis to invade Cuba and eliminate Castro. Given this assessment, Khrushchev interpreted military preparations as expressions of intention and took very seriously the likelihood of an attack against the Soviet Union as well as Cuba.

The American understanding of the Soviet political system was equally flawed. Although scholars and policymakers alike recognized that Khrushchev did not exercise as much dictatorial power as his ruthless predecessor, they nevertheless exaggerated his ability to control Soviet foreign policy at every level. The president and his advisors were correspondingly insensitive to the possibility that any Soviet action could be unauthorized or reflect poor coordination and inadequate guidance from above. In a totalitarian dictatorship, they reasoned, all political and military actions were carefully orchestrated components of a policy formulated and directed by the central leadership. Nobody in the White House could conceive of the possibility that the Soviet military had shot down a U-2 over Cuba without Khrushchev's knowledge or permission and that the Soviet leader was as horrified as they were to learn of the incident.

The context of bargaining is also determined by its asymmetries, and when the parties involved assess those asymmetries differently, they are likely to misinterpret one another's signals. International relations once again provides an example: the Sino-Indian border dispute that led to war between the two countries in October 1962.

The contest over the territories, the Aksai Chin in the west and the Tawang Tract in the east, was the result of ill-defined colonial frontiers in the Himalayas. China sought a compromise solution; India laid claim to all the territory. To strengthen its position, India sent patrols into the disputed and largely inaccessible territories during 1961–62. After repeated warnings to India to refrain from provocative military maneuvers, China ordered its forces to surround the newly established Indian outposts in Ladakh, in the west. Having demonstrated their ability to cut off these outposts, the Chinese withdrew, leaving Indian forces unharmed. Beijing intended its action as a demonstration of resolve, and one that would allow Indian leaders to back down without loss of face, because of its nonviolent nature. Officials in New Delhi interpreted the Chinese withdrawal as a sign of timidity. India's leaders accordingly became bolder in their efforts to occupy as much of the disputed territory, east and west, as possible. In the face of these provocations, China launched a well-coordinated attack and quickly overran Indian positions on both fronts.

The Sino-Indian misunderstanding was the result of diametrically opposed estimates of the relative strengths of the two countries. China's leaders were convinced of their country's military advantage in the disputed territories and hoped that restraint on their part might encourage a more compromising attitude in New Delhi. But India's leaders thought that their country had the advantage and interpreted China's restraint as lack of resolve. The flawed assessment of the military balance held by Prime Minister Nehru and Foreign Minister Menon was the result of a series of self-serving and unrealistic intelligence reports from India's highly politicized army. The Chinese, who formulated their estimates on the basis of more thorough and professional analyses of the military capabilities of the two sides, had no way of knowing the extent to which the Indian leadership was misinformed.

In Cuba, misunderstanding paradoxically contributed to resolution of the crisis. Each side exaggerated the other's resolve and hastened to make the concessions it thought necessary for an accommodation. Misunderstandings more often confound agreement, as happened in the Falklands and the Sino-Indian disputes, where Argentina, Britain and India all underestimated their opponent's resolve. Some of these estimates of risk were shaped by noise or stereotypes of the other side. Other faulty estimates were the result of misunderstood signals, and those misunderstandings arose because signals were formulated and interpreted in different contexts.

For all these reasons, barriers to effective signaling and problems in fathoming another party's preferences can combine to make punishment and reward unpredictable strategies. Parties who use these strategies need to be aware of their limitations, the kinds of situations in which they are likely to run into trouble by using them, and what can be done to improve their chances for success. It is to this last consideration that we now direct our attention.

Chapter 13

Setting Things Straight

The previous chapter identified three impediments to successful implementation of the strategies of punishment and rewards: opaque preferences, signaling problems, and different understandings of the context. Opaque preferences make the consequences of threats and promises unpredictable. Barriers to effective signaling make threats and promises difficult to communicate and to make credible. Different understandings of context encourage different expectations about the terms of agreement; they are also a root cause of signaling problems.

The first step in overcoming any of these impediments is to recognize their existence. Sensitivity to them, their consequences, and the kinds of situations in which they are encountered makes a bargainer more likely to spot problems in time to initiate corrective action.

The second step in coping requires some understanding of the cognitive and motivational roots of all three impediments. Cognition and motivation mediate understanding of context and determine receptivity to information. They also determine the concepts and analogies used to frame problems, the responses deemed relevant to them, and expectations about their consequences.

Cognition is subject to many distortions. People use misleading analogies to interpret information, make false inferences about the motives or constraints influencing other actors, and miscalculate the probabilities of outcomes. Cognitive distortions are innocent, in the sense that people have no emotional commitment to them. New information, especially when it is dramatically at variance with beliefs or expectations, can prompt their reassessment. In 1992 and 1993, the American intelligence community advised President Clinton that North Korea's refusal to allow inspectors from the International Atomic Energy Agency (IAEA) to examine suspected reprocessing facilities was an attempt to extract economic and political concessions. North Korea was offered economic rewards if it allowed inspections and brought its policies in line with IAEA procedures. North Korea's repeated refusal to do this, and its withdrawal from the IAEA in June 1993, forced the United States, Japan, and South Korea to reassess their policies and reframe the problem. North Korea, they concluded, was committed to the development of nuclear weapons and missile delivery systems and could only be stopped by economic sanctions or military action. A year later, North Korean diplomatic overtures following the death of Kim Il-sung, renewed hopes that some kind of accommodation might be reached. After intense negotiations, an agreement was hammered out in which North Korea agreed to stop reprocessing nuclear fuel, rejoin the IAEA, and permit inspections, in return for economic aid and new reactors. In the course of this rapidly evolving situation, American beliefs about North Korean motives changed twice in response to new information.

Motivational biases are more intractable. They reflect strong emotional needs to maintain a particular construction of reality and are more resistant, and sometimes altogether impervious, to discrepant information. Studies reveal that committed smokers are much less likely than nonsmokers to give credence to information about the harmful effects of tobacco. Smokers who are unwilling or unable to quit tend to ignore, deny, distort, discredit, or explain away such information or insist that it does not apply to them. To overcome motivational biases, it is often necessary to deal with the underlying causes of the bias. This can be very difficult, especially in the short term. Most of the suggestions that follow are accordingly aimed at reducing cognitive barriers to bargaining.

Opaque Preferences

Preferences are sometimes transparent. Bargainers may be forthright about their goals, or their goals may be easy to infer from the context. On other occasions preferences are not so clear. Bargainers frequently try to conceal them. A bargainer who needs to satisfy an important constituency may try to keep its dependence on that third party a secret, to prevent it from being exploited by the other side. The other side's preferences may appear to be transparent but in fact be hidden.

You need to proceed cautiously. At the outset, estimate the other side's preferences and rank them. This estimate should then be tested against the party's behavior. If the behavior proves consistent with the estimate, you can gradually invest more confidence in the estimate. If not, with what set of preferences does it appear consistent? Always treat initial estimates of preferences as speculative, provisional, and unverified. When you are unclear or uncertain about the other side's preferences, you should be wary about offering rewards or making threats whose success depends on an accurate understanding of preferences.

Preference estimation need not be passive. You can try to elicit information from the other side about its preferences. As a general rule, bargainers will be more forthcoming when they trust you, see you as committed to accommodation, and are facing complicated bargaining situations in which some kind of coordination is essential. In these circumstances, it may be possible to treat the bargaining encounter as a coordination problem. If this succeeds, both sides stand to gain. If not, promises and threats can be used to overcome the differences that the attempt at coordination has brought to light.

In situations characterized by no-holds-barred bargaining, the other side may still be willing to provide some information about its preferences. It may want to dramatize the importance of particular demands or make its threats more credible. It may also provide information if it suspects that you misunderstand it and that more accurate information might elicit a more appropriate and attractive offer. You should consider providing information to the other side about your preferences to prevent misunderstanding on its part and to solicit information in return. An exchange of information may be in the interest of both sides.

For all of these reasons it is useful to encourage others to be open about their preferences. Any information you glean may provide the basis for a better and more successful choice of strategies. It may permit the design of more potent threats or more attractive incentives to move the other side toward concessions. Alternatively, it may indicate why threats or promises under consideration are unlikely to succeed.

When the other side is unwilling to discuss its preferences, it must of necessity provide some information about them if an accommodation is to be reached. At the very least, it must accept or reject your offers. A lot can be learned from the substance of offers and counteroffers, as well as from public and private statements by the parties involved.

The Arab response to Israel's deportation of four hundred Hamas activists in December 1992 offers a good example of how to read between the lines of a party's behavior. The Palestine Liberation Organization insisted that the Middle East peace talks be deferred until the deportees were allowed to go home. Syria, Egypt, and Saudi Arabia rejected this appeal and urged the PLO to return to the negotiating table. President Hafez el-Assad of Syria, one of the principal parties to the negotiations, insisted that bigger issues were at stake. Israeli leaders could properly infer that Syria was more interested in the return of the Golan Heights than in the fate of the Palestinians. Saudi Arabia resumed subsidies to the PLO in an effort to persuade its leader, Yasir Arafat, to participate in the negotiations. The Saudis' behavior made it apparent that they too were anxious for a general settlement of the Arab-Israeli conflict.

People sometimes provide subtle, unintentional clues about their preferences, vulnerabilities, and needs. Their agendas, body language, choice of words, and emotional states communicate important information. In 1991, I went to the Ismalovsky Market in Moscow in search of an icon. This was not my first trip, and I was known to several dealers. One of them rushed out from behind his booth to greet me. His ill-concealed pleasure at seeing me belied his claim that business was good and that there were many tourists in town willing to pay top dollar for quality icons. Good bargainers, like good poker players, control their emotions, and send out only signals of their choosing. They are alert to the signals of others, learn to distinguish between intent and bluff, and when possible, use signals others send to read their hands.

Clever bargainers try to get inside information about others' preferences. Friends, associates, disgruntled employees, and spies can provide critical intelligence about the motives and objectives of the other side. For many years Soviet spy Richard Sorge cultivated contacts in the Japanese defense ministry. In late 1940, he learned that the Japanese military considered the United States and the European colonial powers stronger and more threatening than the Soviet Union. Japan would therefore attack to the south and west, rather than east into Soviet Siberia. On the basis of Sorge's reports, Stalin denuded Siberia of troops and rushed them to Moscow in time to save the city from the advancing Germans.

Spies of the quality of Sorge are few and far between—and poor Sorge was discovered and hanged by the Japanese. Spies place the broader relationship between parties at risk; accordingly, they need to be used with caution. Other inside sources of information are more practical.

Signaling Problems

Problems of signaling are primarily a function of context. They are least likely to occur when communication is conducted through long-established channels and uses forms well understood by the bargainers. Auctions at Sotheby's and trading on major stock exchanges are cases in point. The participants share a complex lexicon of signals and know from experience the meaning and nuances associated with each of them. Despite the commotion and seeming chaos on the floor of many stock exchanges, the signal-to-noise ratio is remarkably high.

Signaling problems are most likely to occur when bargainers come from different cultures and their relationship is hostile. Cultural barriers make it more likely that parties will frame and interpret signals in different contexts, leading to the kinds of problems described in the previous chapter. Hostility and anger distort signals for different reasons. They prompt bargainers to put the worst possible interpretation on each other's behavior. Signals of moderation and reconciliation may be missed or misinterpreted.

Cultural barriers to signaling are most obvious in international relations, where leaders from different political systems with different personal backgrounds who speak different languages must nevertheless communicate with precision. These barriers also exist within countries and between organizations that give the appearence of cultural homogeneity. In the 1970s, I was professor of strategy at the National War College in Washington, D.C., and would arrange for guest speakers to address the colonels, navy captains, and civilian officials who formed our student body. One unusually interesting and articulate presentation on arms control by the then assistant secretary of state for political-military affairs triggered a series of questions cum accusations that the speaker had repeatedly contradicted himself. I was baffled by this response until I realized that the assistant secretary, a Jewish New Yorker, had relied on sarcasm and irony to communicate disbelief and scorn. His words had been taken at face value by a predominantly white southern audience unaccustomed to this style of discourse.

Hostility and anger also interfere with communication. George Bush's response to the Iraqi invasion of Kuwait was intensely personal and transformed an interstate dispute into an eyeball-to-eyeball confrontation between himself and Saddam Hussein. Hostility and anger are much more likely to dominate interpersonal bargaining. Divorces and disputes between neighbors and business partners are notorious for their emotional intensity and the inability of the protagonists, who were once quite close, to communicate. In such intense encounters, it is often more effective to negotiate through third parties. Sometimes, these go-betweens find it easier to communicate and bargain with each other than they do with their respective clients. Divorce lawyers frequently complain that it is more difficult to convince a husband or wife to approve an agreement than it is to negotiate it.

There are a number of time-honored techniques for communicating more effectively:

Subtle signals. Avoid subtle signals, which are based on distinctions that are obvious to the sender but often obscure to the receiver. A striking example is the U.S. decision in 1965 to send ashore a "light" Marine division instead of a more fully armed "heavy" Army division. This was intended to signal North Vietnam that the Johnson administration had limited military objectives. The political significance of the two types of forces was lost on Hanoi, for whom the salient fact was the deployment. Later in the war, target selection and bombing pauses were used to convey complex messages. There is no evidence that they succeeded.

Sending a light rather than heavy division failed as a signal because it was an attempt to piggyback a subtle signal (about the limits of U.S. involvement) on a blunt and dramatic signal (military intervention in Vietnam). The latter signal received all the attention. This signal and many others sent by Washington during the Indochinese conflict failed because the North Vietnamese did not regard force structures, bombing targets, and bombing pauses as symbolic forms of communication but as tactical responses to military exigencies. For signals to succeed, targets must recognize them for what they are *and* understand the context in which they are framed. It is often better to rely on blunt signals that exploit shared contexts; more nuanced messages are likely to be missed or misunderstood.

Multiple channels. The more often a signal is repeated and the more diverse the channels used to transmit it, the more likely it is to be recognized and understood. The "shotgun" approach to signaling assumes that a message delivered by many sources will achieve greater salience and more attention. The advertising industry is based on this principle, and market studies reveal a significant correlation between consumer choice and exposure to a product. You should consider employing this technique in situations where you suspect your signal may be dismissed as noise.

Shared channels. Messages are more likely to be recognized when they are sent through anticipated channels. People often associate important communications with specific routines or practices. College couples may place seemingly cryptic personal announcements in small print in the back pages of school newspapers. Their parents may go to a particular restaurant for dinner to signal that they have something important to discuss. Business partners hold retreats or extraordinary staff meetings, and heads of state exploit trusted "back channels" to convey particularly important messages. Use of such symbolic channels imparts special salience to the message. It also places a corresponding responsibility on those who employ such channels to use them wisely. In the eighteen months before the Cuban missile crisis, President Kennedy and Soviet premier Nikita Khrushchev used Georgiy N. Bol'shakov, a KGB officer, to convey private letters between them. The letters addressed a number of delicate issues including Laos, Berlin, and plans for a Vienna summit. Kennedy had come to rely on this back channel and was deeply offended that Khrushchev used it to deceive him about his intentions to deploy missiles in Cuba. After the Soviet missiles were discovered, Bol'shakov lost his credibility and the two leaders were left without any trusted, private channel of communication.

Symbolic channels work best when they are used sparingly and for messages to which you want to impart special salience. Their value declines if they are used too often or for inappropriate purposes.

Shared contexts. Messages need to be understood as well as recognized. This is much more likely when sender and recipient use the same context to frame and interpret them. Skillful communicators try to choose contexts or points of reference they expect recipients to share and understand. They also try to put a message in context by using analogies or language that supplies the context for those to whom it is addressed.

In the fall of 1949, shortly after the communist victory in China's civil war, Mao Zedong traveled to Moscow to confer with Soviet leaders. Joseph Stalin held a banquet in his honor and asked what the Soviet Union could do to help their Chinese comrades. Mao replied, "We expect to create something that should not only look nice but taste delicious." Stalin and Beria, chief of the secret police, were baffled, and in subsequent meetings tried and failed to elicit from Mao just what he wanted. The communication problem was overcome only when the more worldly Zhou Enlai was summoned to Moscow. He eschewed metaphor for the more prosaic language of diplomacy.

Professional communicators. Law and diplomacy are much-maligned professions. Some lawyers and diplomats perform critical functions. They serve as credible and effective go-betweens, explaining the interests and positions of their clients or governments to other clients or governments. Training and experience have honed their interpersonal skills and ability to empathize and communicate. Lawyers and diplomats also benefit in negotiation from knowing the special languages and norms of their professions and from the degree of trust that often exists between opposing lawyers or diplomats by virtue of their personal relationships or professional reputations.

Lawyers and diplomats must nevertheless be used with caution. They can needlessly complicate a situation or unwittingly misrepresent you. They also have interests of their own. Lawyers need to think about problems in terms of hours and fees. Diplomats can "go local" and give too much importance to the interests or worldview of the countries to which they are accredited. However, in situations where the principals find it difficult to speak to one another, because of cultural or personal differences, professional communicators can be of great value. They can also provide useful advice or assistance on the conduct of negotiations.

Reduced hostility. Making antagonists more responsive to each other's communications and interests often requires lowering the tension between them. Many couples communicate best after fighting, or making love, or both. Confrontation, when limited to verbal combat, allows a couple to let off steam and express hostility. Lovemaking brings them back together and emphasizes their common bonds and affection.

Business leaders, governmental officials, and statesmen generally avoid this kind of intimacy with their opposite numbers. There are other well-established techniques they can use to disengage emotions and promote a calmer assessment of the problem and greater empathy. These include agreeing on "cooling-off" periods, during which both sides let an issue sit unresolved for a while; structured encounters, by which they can give vent to their anger within carefully controlled bounds; seminars and other activities to bring parties together in circumstances that promote more cooperative relationships; and the use of trusted go-betweens to explain the positions and grievances of each side to the other. In relationships characterized by hostility and tension, it is often advisable to employ such techniques before addressing any substantive issues.

Different Understandings of Context

President Kennedy's September 1962 warnings to the Soviet Union not to deploy offensive weapons in Cuba have been described as a textbook example of responsible diplomacy. The warnings were communicated publicly and privately, in words and in writing, by the president and other top officials, to Soviet premier Khrushchev, his foreign minister, and the Soviet ambassador to Washington. Some of the private communications made it clear that offensive weapons included any missiles capable of attacking the American mainland. The use of repetition and multiple channels succeeded in conveying Kennedy's message to Khrushchev, but these techniques did not influence his behavior. Khrushchev did not understand why Kennedy found the prospect of Soviet missiles in Cuba so threatening. He convinced himself that if the deployment could be kept secret until after the November congressional elections, the Americans would do nothing more than lodge verbal protests.

Like many of the other unsuccessful signals described in the last chapter, Kennedy's warnings failed because their target had a very different understanding of the context of their bargaining encounter. Khrushchev might have responded differently if he had understood the full extent of public pressure on Kennedy to overthrow Castro, and how Cuba had become the political Achilles heel of the Kennedy administration because of its failure at the Bay of Pigs. For his part, Kennedy misunderstood the context in which Khrushchev viewed Cuba. He was convinced that deployment of the missiles indicated Khrushchev's doubt of his resolve and that failure to honor his commitment to keep Soviet missiles out of Cuba would invite a new and more serious challenge in Berlin. Khrushchev was largely oblivious to these concerns; his attention was focused on the domestic and foreign problems that a missile deployment might help him resolve.

Motivational bias interfered with Khrushchev's understanding of Kennedy's context. The Soviet premier was driven by domestic and foreign needs to send missiles to Cuba. Because he needed to believe that the missile deployment would succeed, he made no effort to look at the problem from Kennedy's perspective. He brushed aside warnings from several of his advisors that the missiles were likely to be discovered by the Americans and provoke a serious crisis. Other important causes of contextual misunderstandings, described in the previous chapter, are inaccurate information, inadequate information, and mirror imaging. All of them blind bargainers to the perspectives of others.

As with opaque preferences, the first step in coping with contextual misunderstandings is to recognize their prevalence. A conscious effort must be made to reconstruct the other side's understanding of the bargaining situation. How does it frame the problem? What does it think is at stake? What asymmetries does it consider important, and whom does it think they favor? What kind of outcome does it expect? Provisional answers to these questions can be gleaned from that actor's past behavior and from public and private communications about the bargaining situation and the issues involved, on and off the table.

Information of this kind can sometimes be obtained directly from the other side. One or both sides may be eager to communicate their understanding of context to justify their interests and demands. If Argentina had been able to persuade Britain to accept its definition of the Falklands dispute as a colonial problem, it would have derived a substantial bargaining advantage. If China had been able to convince India that its forces were at a significant military disadvantage in all of the disputed territories, Nehru and Menon might have pursued a more accommodative strategy. Both these conflicts are examples of signaling problems arising not only because one or the other party fails to explain its understanding of context but because one side fails to listen or treat seriously the explanations offered by the other.

This problem points to a common cognitive failure. Once people have framed a problem, they are reluctant to consider other ways of viewing it, and they resist information that cannot easily be assimilated into their frame of reference. Good signaling is a two-way street. You must convey your understanding of context to others if they are to recognize and correctly interpret your signals. You must recognize the possibility—even more likely in conflictual situations—that the other side will frame the problem and understand the context differently. You must remain open to efforts by others to explain their understanding of the situation.

The problem of context has implications that go beyond signaling. Conflicting understandings of context can make it impossible to find a zone of agreement. When both sides have different interpretations of asymmetries, they will develop different expectations about what constitutes a reasonable agreement. If each side believes it has more at stake, more resources, and will benefit from the passage of time, it will insist on a more favorable outcome. Two bargainers demanding settlements skewed in their favor does not make for agreement.

Very occasionally, contrasting interpretations of asymmetries facilitate agreement. If each side concludes that time is working against it, or that the other side has more resources, both may be more willing to reach an accommodation. The Anti-Ballistic Missile (ABM) Treaty of 1972 was the result of Soviet and American estimates that the other superpower was ahead in the development of ballistic missile defenses. Each wanted a treaty to constrain the other. Agreement is most difficult to reach when two sides believe that key asymmetries work in their favor. In such situations, successful bargaining may require the bargainers to develop more of a shared understanding of the bargaining context. Only then may a zone of agreement emerge.

In some bargaining encounters mutual exchange of information may be sufficient to shift the estimates one or both bargainers have of the relevant asymmetries. In negotiations over dumping of goods, for example, several Pacific Rim countries denied that their manufacturers were guilty of such practices and tried to stonewall American demands for tighter controls. American negotiators were able to provide convincing documentation of their accusations and thereby compel the governments in question to recognize the severity of the problem. Once these countries had altered their estimates of the asymmetries, they became more pliable in the negotiations. In other situations, bargainers resist the implications of new information if accepting them would undercut their bargaining advantages or strategies. In the Mutual Balanced Force Reduction negotiations, the Soviets for many years rejected American estimates of Warsaw Pact force levels in Eastern Europe and offered numbers that both sides knew to be unreasonably low. The negotiations made no progress until the late 1980s, when Soviet representatives accepted the Western figures. They did so because Moscow's political agenda had changed and General Secretary Mikhail Gorbachev and his advisors regarded an agreement as in their interests.

Hard bargaining and perseverance may sometimes be required to bring about a common understanding of the context. This kind of prebargaining may nevertheless be necessary to create the framework in which subsequent agreement on substantive issues will be possible. Bargainers must be sensitive to this problem and try to structure a common framework within which to address contextual questions *before* tackling substantive ones.

Afterword

We have proceeded step by step, from consideration of the utility of bargaining to the setting of goals and choice of strategies, to selling an
agreement to important constituencies, to gaining support for its implementation. For purposes of analysis, it made sense to treat these choices
and operations as sequential and distinct. In practice, this is rarely the case.

Many choices and operations overlap. Experienced bargainers may
explore the feasibility of bargaining, develop alternatives, try to manipulate others' understanding of the bargaining context, and think about the
best way of handling a dominant constituency all at the same time. Their
choices about any of these issues are almost certain to influence their
choices about others. A judgment that a dominant constituency can be
won over to some outcomes but not to others may influence the decision
of whether bargaining is feasible; it might also suggest appropriate bargaining strategies. A favorable asymmetry might dictate a strategy that in
turn requires isolation of a constituency. Although our narrative treated
bargaining as a progression, it is better represented as a series of feedback
loops. Choices and operations not only overlap, they are interdependent.

Our focus on structure and process obscured another elemental truth
of bargaining: the important role of experience and skill. Simulations and
studies of real world encounters indicate that the ability of the negotiators
makes an enormous difference. Bargainers with good interpersonal skills
and a finely honed strategic sense can negotiate better deals and reach

agreements when others cannot. They are also more likely to recognize beforehand situations in which bargaining is likely to fail.

To some degree, good bargainers are born, not made. But a conceptual understanding of bargaining, lots of experience, and reflection about that experience can improve any bargainer's skill.

Bibliography

Bacharach, Samuel B., and Edward J. Lawler. "Power Dependence and Power Paradoxes in Bargaining." *Negotiation Journal,* April 1986, pp. 167–75.

Beirsteker, Thomas. "Knowledge versus Ignorance as Bargaining Strategies: The Impact of Knowledge about Other's Information Level." *Social Science Journal* 26, no. 2 (1989), pp. 161–72.

Bell, David V. J. "Political Linguistics and International Negotiation." *International Organization* 4, no. 3 (July 1988), pp. 233–46.

Bercovitch, Jacob. "Problems and Approaches in the Study of Bargaining and Negotiation." *Political Science* 36, no. 2 (December 1984), pp. 125–44.

Bueno de Mesquita, Bruce. "Multilateral Negotiations: A Spatial Analysis of the Arab-Israeli Dispute." *International Organization* 44, no. 3 (summer 1990), pp. 317–40.

Caporaso, James A. "International Relations Theory and Multilateralism: The Search for Foundations." *International Organization* 46, no. 3 (summer 1992), pp. 599–632.

Downie, Bryan. "When Negotiations Fail: Causes of Breakdown and Tactics for Breaking the Stalemate." *Negotiation Journal,* April 1991, pp. 175–86.

Druckman, Daniel, ed. *Negotiations: Social-Psychological Perspectives.* Beverly Hills, Calif.: Sage, 1977.

Druckman, Daniel. "Turning Points in the INF Negotiations." *Negotiation Journal* 7, no. 1 (January 1991), pp. 55–68.

Faure, G. O., and J. Z. Rubin, eds. *Culture and Negotiation.* Beverly Hills, Calif.: Sage, 1993.

Griffiths, Franklyn. "Limits of the Tabular View of Negotiation." *International Journal* 35 (winter 1979–80), pp. 33–46.

Gulliver, P. H. *Disputes and Negotiations: A Cross-Cultural Perspective.* New York: Academic Press, 1979.

Hampson, Fen Osler, with Michael Hart. *Multilateral Negotiations: Lessons from Arms Control, Trade, and the Environment.* Baltimore: Johns Hopkins University Press, 1995.

Higgott, Richard A., and Andrew F. Cooper. "Middle Power Leadership and Coalition Building: Australia, the Cairns Group and the Uruguay Round of

Trade Negotiations." *International Organization* 44, no. 4 (autumn 1990), pp. 591–632.

Kahler, Miles. "Multilateralism with Small and Large Numbers." *International Organization* 46, no. 3 (summer 1992), pp. 681–708.

Kahneman, Daniel. "Reference Points, Anchors, Norms, and Mixed Feelings." *Organizational Behavior and Human Decision Processes* 51 (1992), pp. 296–312.

Kremenyuk, Victor A., ed. *International Negotiation: Analysis, Approaches, Issues.* San Francisco: Jossey-Bass, 1991.

Larson, Deborah Welch. "The Psychology of Reciprocity in Diplomatic Negotiations." *International Organization* 4, no. 3 (July 1988), pp. 281–302.

Lax, David A., and James K. Sebenius. *The Manager as Negotiator: Bargaining for Cooperation and Competitive Gain.* New York: Free Press, 1986; London: Collier Macmillan, 1986.

Lebow, Richard Ned, and Janice Gross Stein. *We All Lost the Cold War.* Princeton: Princeton University Press, 1994. Used for all references to the Cuban missile crisis and the October 1973 war in the Middle East.

Martin, Geoffrey R. "The 'Practical' and the 'Theoretical' Split in Modern Negotiation Literature." *Negotiation Journal* 4, no. 1 (January 1988), pp. 45–54.

Martin, Lisa L. "Interests, Power, and Multilateralism." *International Organization* 46, no. 4 (autumn 1992), pp. 765–92.

Mautner-Markhof, Frances. *Processes of International Negotiation.* Boulder, Colo.: Westview Press, 1989.

Murray, John S. "Understanding Competing Theories of Negotiation." *Negotiation Journal* 2, no. 2 (April 1986), pp. 179–86.

Neale, Margaret A., and Max B. Bazerman. "Perspectives for Understanding Negotiation." *Journal of Conflict Resolution* 29, no. 1 (March 1985), pp. 33–55.

Pruitt, Dean G. *Negotiation Behavior.* New York: Academic Press, 1981.

Pruitt, Dean G., and Peter J. Carnevale. *Negotiation in Social Conflict.* Pacific Grove, Calif.: Brooks Cole, 1993.

Putnam, Robert D. "Diplomacy and Domestic Politics: The Logic of Two-Level Games." *International Organization* 42, no. 3 (summer 1988), pp. 427–60.

Raiffa, Howard. *The Art and Science of Negotiation.* Cambridge: Harvard University Press, 1982.

Rothstein, Robert L. "Regime-Creation by a Coalition of the Weak: Lessons from the NIEO and the Integrated Program for Commodities." *International Studies Quarterly* 28, no. 3 (1984), pp. 307–28.

Rubin, Jeffrey, and Bert Brown. *The Social Psychology of Bargaining and Negotiation.* New York: Academic Press, 1975.

Ruggie, John. "Multilateralism." *International Organization* 46, no. 3 (summer 1992), pp. 561–98.

Schelling, Thomas C. *The Strategy of Conflict.* Cambridge: Harvard University Press, 1960.

Sebenius, James K. *Negotiating the Law of the Sea: Lessons in the Art and Science of Reaching Agreement.* Cambridge: Harvard University Press, 1984.

Sebenius, James K. "Negotiation Analysis: A Characterization and Review." *Management Science* 38 (January 1992), pp. 18–38.

Sebenius, James K. "Negotiation Arithmetic: Adding and Subtracting Issues and Parties." *International Organization* 37 (spring 1983), pp. 281–316.

Sjöstedt, G., B. Spector, and I. W. Zartman, eds. *Negotiating International Regimes.* London: Graham and Trotman, 1994.

Sloss, Leon, and M. Scott Davis, eds. *A Game for High Stakes: Lessons Learned in Negotiating with the Soviet Union.* Cambridge, Mass.: Ballinger, 1986.

Stein, Janice Gross, ed. *Getting to the Table: The Processes of Prenegotiation.* Baltimore: Johns Hopkins University Press, 1989.

Stein, Janice Gross. "International Negotiation: A Multidisciplinary Perspective." *Negotiation Journal* 4, no. 3 (July 1988), pp. 211–20.

Stein, Janice Gross, and Louis W. Pauly. *Choosing to Cooperate: How States Avoid Loss.* Baltimore: Johns Hopkins University Press, 1993.

Weiss, Stephen E. "Negotiating with 'Romans,'" parts 1 and 2. *Sloan Management Review,* nos. 2 and 3 (winter 1994).

Winham, Gilbert R. "Multilateral Economic Negotiation." *Negotiation Journal* 3, no. 2 (April 1987), pp. 175–90.

Winham, Gilbert R. "Negotiation as a Management Process." *World Politics* 30, no. 1 (July 1977), pp. 87–114.

Young, H. Peyton. *Negotiation Analysis.* Ann Arbor: University of Michigan Press, 1991.

Young, Oran R., ed. *Bargaining: Formal Theories of Negotiation.* Urbana: University of Illinois Press, 1975.

Young, Oran R. "The Politics of International Regime Formation: Managing Natural Resources and the Environment." *International Organization* 34, no. 3 (summer 1989), pp. 349–76.

Zartman, I. William. "Common Elements in the Analysis of the Negotiation Process." *Negotiation Journal* 4, no. 1 (January 1988), pp. 31–43.

Zartman, I. William, ed. *International Multilateral Negotiations: Approaches to the Management of Complexity.* New York: Jossey-Bass, 1994.

Zartman, I. William. *Many Are Called but Few Choose: The Analysis of Multilateral Negotiations.* Project on international negotiation of the International Institute of Applied Systems Analysis, Vienna, Austria, forthcoming.

Zartman, I. William. *Positive Sum: Improving North-South Negotiations.* New Brunswick, N.J.: Transaction Books, 1987.

Index

Library of Congress Cataloging-in-Publication Data

Lebow, Richard Ned.
  The art of bargaining / Richard Ned Lebow.
    p.   cm.
  Includes bibliographical references (p.   ) and index.
  ISBN 0-8018-5198-X (hard : alk. paper)
  1. Diplomatic negotiations in international disputes.   I. Title.
JX4473.L43 1996
341.5'22—dc20   95-31502